A. H. Ritchie

HER WAYS ARE WAYS OF PLEASANTNESS

Prov 3. & 17.

PLEASANT PATHWAYS

Daniel Wise

A. H. Ritchie.

MAHMOUD THE IDOL BREAKER.

Pg. 44.

PLEASANT PATHWAYS;

OR,

'ERSUASIVES TO EARLY PIETY:

CONTAINING

EXPLANATIONS AND ILLUSTRATIONS OF THE BEAUTY, SAFETY, AND PLEASANTNESS OF A RELIGIOUS LIFE:

BEING

AN EARNEST ATTEMPT TO PERSUADE YOUNG PEOPLE OF BOTH SEXES TO SEEK HAPPINESS IN THE LOVE AND SERVICE OF JESUS CHRIST.

By DANIEL WISE,

AUTHOR OF "THE PATH OF LIFE," "YOUNG MAN'S COUNSELOR," ETC., ETC.

"Her ways are ways of pleasantness, and all her paths are peace."

NINTH THOUSAND.

New York:

PUBLISHED BY CARLTON & PORTER,

200 MULBERRY-STREET.

Inscription.

TO THE

YOUNG PEOPLE OF AMERICA GENERALLY,

BUT PARTICULARLY TO THOSE WHOSE EARLY YEARS HAVE BEEN BLESSED WITH THE PIOUS INSTRUCTIONS OF A GODLY HOME AND OF A CHRISTIAN SUNDAY SCHOOL,

THIS WORK

IS AFFECTIONATELY INSCRIBED BY THEIR SINCERE FRIEND AND WELL-WISHER,

DANIEL WISE.

PREFACE.

There are many excellent books in the world, written for the purpose of leading young people into the way of peace. They all have their mission, and are all contributing their meed of help in preparing our youth to be polished stones in the Lord's build ing. Yet inasmuch as many of them are written in a spirit so stern, or in a style so grave, as to be without attraction sufficient to command the attention of *unawakened* youth generally, I have long thought that a volume, made attractive by the abundance and interest of its illustrations, yet dealing pungently with the conscience, and appealing faithfully to the hopes and fears of the young mind, might be instrumental in reaching some erring but precious young souls who are inaccessible to the influence of kindred works. This conviction led me to plan and to commence this book some six years ago. My editorial and other duties hindered its completion, until, moved by daily reflection on the brevity and uncertainty of life, and by a desire to plead in Christ's behalf with as many of the youth of my times as possible, I employed the spare moments of the past year in bringing it to a conclusion. That I have reached the height of my purpose, or equaled the excellence of Baxter, Alleine, Doddridge, or Pike, I have not the vanity to presume; that I have sincerely attempted to win some jewels for my Master's crown from among the millions of our great nation's youth, I am clearly conscious. With this consciousness, I send forth my unpretending book—a modest messenger of love—praying that it may be an evangel to many hearts, and the guide of thousands into "ways of pleasantness and paths of peace." D. W.

233 Adelphi-street, Brooklyn,
January, 1859.

CONTENTS

CHAPTER I.

THE BUBBLE BURST.

CHAPTER II.

HOW TO ENJOY THIS LIFE.

CHAPTER III.

SOCIAL HAZARDS OF A SINFUL LIFE.

CHAPTER IV.

LINKED ARMOR FOR TEMPTED YOUNG SOULS.

CHAPTER V.

THE DARK DAYS OF LIFE.

CHAPTER VI.

PLEASURES PECULIAR TO PIETY.

CHAPTER VII.

HOW TO WIN VICTORY IN DEATH.

CHAPTER VIII.

LIFE BEYOND THE GRAVE.

CHAPTER IX.

I PRAY THEE HAVE ME EXCUSED.

CHAPTER X.

THE PROCRASTINATOR'S DOOM.

CHAPTER XI.

VOICES OF DUTY.

CHAPTER XII.

WHAT SHALL I DO BE SAVED?

CHAPTER XIII.

THE FAITH THAT SAVES US.

PLEASANT PATHWAYS.

CHAPTER I.

THE BUBBLE BURST.

A CELEBRATED and highly popular comedian once waited upon a physician with a request to be cured of an overpowering melancholy. "Go," advised the medical gentleman, "go to the theater and witness the comic performances of ——"

"Alas!" replied his patient, "I am that comedian! I make others merry, but, while they are laughing at the sallies of my wit, my own heart is as unmoved as a stone. Amid the laughter of delighted multitudes I remain the most sad and miserable of beings myself!"

How true to the experience of all worldlings is this picture of the comedian's heart! He was a hypocrite in his pleasantries: so are all gay sinners. Their eyes flash, their lips smile, their tongues utter sparkling jests, but their hearts silently sigh over a conscious vacuity which they vainly implore the world to fill. Their consciences sting them for degrading spiritual capacities, capable of grasping the Infinite, to the Dead Sea of sensuality, and for casting away eternal life at the bidding of bodily appetites and passions. But in vain does the soul sigh and the conscience sting. The sinner will have his delights. He hides his misery. He dances, sings, jests; his merry laugh rings through the air, and his companions in sin, wondering, think him happy. They will not believe his laugh, like theirs, is sepulchral, and therefore they envy him his felicity. He too, in his turn, is deceived by the merriment of his companions, and envies them. Thus, all envy, all laugh, all are deceived; all are hypocrites in their sinful pleasantries.

Start not, dear reader, from this image of your heart! The fault is not in my mirror but in your character. The most ill-featured person is willing to gaze upon his own face in the glass, and surely you will be equally ready to behold your moral features; especially as the hand of a friend holds the mirror, and the motive which prompts him to hold it is the high regard he has for your best interests. If he reveals the strange defeatures sin has wrought upon you, it is only to lead you to One who has power to obliterate them and to cover you with divine beauty; to Him who can fill the vacuum in your heart, silence its sighings, heal its wounds, and who can create a calm, sweet smile upon your lips which shall be the true index of your feelings. Give me, therefore, your hand, your heart, your serious attention, and I will reason with you concerning the things *which make for your peace.*

You have chosen the world. The things of this life are your glory, your delight, your supreme good. Your pleasures, your hopes, your thoughts, all center on the *things which are seen.* You are devoted to the world; yea, chained to it, as the corpse of Hector was bound to the chariot of Achilles on the plain of Troy. You are at once its admirer and its captive, for "*to whom ye yield yourselves servants to obey, his servants ye are.*" Permit me to show you your chosen deity in his true character.

Yonder on the bank of a stream is a little child. He is intently watching the splashing waters as they playfully rush over the pebbles and rocks. Now he dashes at something in the stream. Now he runs along the bank eagerly watching an object which is floating there. How earnest he is! How weary with his long pursuit! Yet onward! *onward still* he descends the brook; now running, now grasping after something which as often eludes his touch. But the day wanes. Night mantles the earth with gloom. The child stops, looks round, and weeps bitterly! The scene is strange to his eyes. He has, in the ardor of his pursuit, wandered far from home! Now that night has come he is weary, faint, *lost!*

What has the child been seeking all day?

He saw a bright *bubble* on the clear waters sparkling in the sunbeam's light. It charmed him. He pursued it. It eluded his grasp, yet still decoyed him down the stream. He sought the worthless thing with all the earnestness of his young heart, missed it, and was lost!

Behold in this child an image of yourself! See in his misfortune a figure of your own ruin! For worthless and false as that bubble is the world you seek. Your enthusiasm in its pursuit is madness. Every step you take leads you farther away from God, the soul's true home, and hurries you toward the region of desolation, sorrow, and death.

"THE WORLD PASSETH AWAY AND THE LUST THEREOF," is an inscription written with the pencil of the Almighty over the archway of the world. The poet has sung, that

"This world is all a fleeting show,
For man's illusion given;
The smiles of joy, the tears of woe,
Deceitful shine, deceitful flow:
There 's nothing true but heaven."

Experience, dearly purchased experience too, has testified to the same effect. It is said that a lady once came suddenly upon an Etrurian monument, in which there was just aperture enough to see, for a moment only, a sitting figure with its look and drapery of more than a thousand years. She beheld it for a few seconds, preserved only in the stillness of antiquity, when *it fell to dust at her very breathing*. Such is the world to its pursuers, beautiful in perspective, *dust* in possession!

These testimonies you now find it difficult to believe. From the gay dreamland of your youth the world appears a scene of unsurpassed loveliness and peerless beauty. You see nothing but bewitching gardens and sunny vales tastefully filled with green trees, gay singing birds warbling delicious music, lovely flowers, and cool fountains glancing in the sunbeams. To these you add multitudes of joyous youth who sport away the flying hours in the highest excitement of unmingled delight. Such to your imagination is the brilliant future of a worldly life!

Alas! alas! My heart is pained at the bare thought of your certain disappointment, for full well I know that these dreams will have no fulfillment. These ideal pictures, created by the enchantments of your fancy, will change to rude, rough, bitter realities, when touched by the wand of that more than magician, Experience. Could I convince you of this, young pilgrim in the journey of life, you might be saved from many an hour of sorrow, perhaps from the jaws of destruction itself. Open your heart, therefore, to conviction, for "*a wise man will hear, and will increase learning; and a man of understanding shall attain unto wise counsels.*"

Suppose, for a moment, that you were suffering very severely from hunger, and were even on the point of actual starvation. In this extremity you look imploringly toward an approaching friend, and with your expiring strength exclaim, "Give me food for pity's sake! I am dying of hunger! Give me something to eat, my friend!"

Your friend, gazing upon you with a pitying eye, promises to bring you instant relief. He hastens away, but speedily returns laden with dusty tomes, the works of the ablest minds and profoundest thinkers among mankind. Throwing them into your arms, he exclaims, "Here, my friend, are some of the finest books extant. They contain the loftiest productions of genius, and teem with the noblest ideas. Feed upon them freely and satisfy your gnawing hunger."

I can easily imagine the look of wonder and indignation with which you would receive this strange communication, and the sharpness of the tone in which you would cry, "Books! Ideas! I want *bread*, not ideas! Who ever heard of ideas being offered to a man in my condition? Sir, if you pity me, give me *bread!*"

Now I contend that such an offer of ideas to satisfy the pains of hunger would be as truly consistent as is your attempt to gratify the wants of your soul with the world. Your friend is supposed to offer *thoughts* —immaterial ideas—to satisfy a *material* or *physical* want. You offer your *spiritual* nature *material* food, and command it to be satisfied! Is not the supposition as consistent as the fact? Is not the one thing as clearly impossible as the other?

Remember, therefore, that the high nature you possess, the spirituality of your inner principle, renders satisfaction in the things of this world impossible. The lofty aspirations, the earnest yearnings of your spiritual nature, will ever turn with unutterable disgust from "*all that is in the world, the lust of the flesh, and the lust of the eyes, and the pride of life,*" as beneath the demands of its infinitely superior capacities. It aspires after communion with the mind of God, it longs to climb eternal heights. Will you doom it to trail its glories in the dust? You may crush its noble aspirings. You may enslave it to the fleshly and the visible, but in so doing you insure its present uneasiness and its eternal misery. Is the world worth the price?

Permit me to bring another illustration to this great question. Imagine yourself bound to take a European voyage. Your residence is some hundred miles or more from the port of embarkation. You gather your outfit, pack your trunks, and take your departure from home. But such has been the confusion attending your preparations, and the excitement of leaving your friends, that, after starting, you find yourself without letters of introduction, and with barely means enough to carry you to the port from whence your vessel is to sail. Now, with this discovery, could you take any real pleasure on your journey? The river boat in which you sailed might be as gorgeous in her appointments and furniture as the palace of an Eastern calif. The scenery around you might be as lovely as the vale of Tempe. The companions of your voyage as cheerful as Mirth. The table furnished with all imaginable delicacies. Yet a thought of your certain embarrassment at the termination of your inland journey would be a frost upon your heart, effectually cooling the ardor of enjoyment. "What shall I do without means or friends?" would be the ghostlike question haunting you every hour, filling you with unrest and alarm.

Do you comprehend my meaning, traveler to the boundless future? know you not that

"Our lives are rivers, gliding free
To that unfathomed, boundless sea,
The silent grave?"

Know you not also that your IMMORTAL SOUL is conscious of wants beyond the quiet tomb? Is it enough to offer that undying nature gifts and goods which *must be left at the grave's mouth?* Granting that your beloved pleasures were sufficiently exalted to meet the present wants of your inner life, yet, gazing on the truth that "*we brought nothing into this world and it is certain* WE CAN CARRY NOTHING OUT," can they give your soul rest? Will not that immortal thing within you often stand gazing into the infinite, beholding the unmeasured cycles of eternity in their stupendous vastness, and feeling an indestructible consciousness that its duration is as unlimited as that eternity? Does not the knowledge that it has no passports, no preparation for that voyage into immensity, cause it to shrink fearfully from its perils? And can the costliest delights of earth quiet its fears or satisfy its desires? Nay! It is impossible! Your immortal nature cries aloud for sources of enjoyment *as enduring as itself.* Give it this world only, and you doom it to disquiet, fear, and sorrow.

What would you say to a man who should seriously declare, "I will hereafter *see* with my *ears* and *hear* with my *eyes!*"

"I should pronounce him a madman," you reply.

"But why call him a madman, my friend?"

"Why, indeed! Could he be less than mad who should pretend to violate the order of God? God has adapted the eye to the nature of light, the ear to the nature of sound, and he must be mad indeed who can *talk* of reversing this method of seeing and hearing. Why, sir, the thing is impossible, the idea madness, the pretension folly!"

All this is true, and proves you, gay worldling, to be a madman indeed. For you are attempting the daring, the impossible folly of violating the order of God! Not, to be sure, in threatening to see with your ears, but in resolving to be happy "*without God.*" As truly as he has appointed the eye to see, the ear to hear, has he also decreed that the soul of man shall find its pleasure in his service. Over the grand archway of human life he has graven this inscription for the guidance of every traveler:

"INCLINE YOUR EAR AND COME UNTO ME:
HEAR AND YOUR SOUL SHALL LIVE."

But you have made a covenant with earthborn pleasure. You have determined "to live" without inclining your ear or coming unto God. In defiance of God's order, and of the established fact that no man has ever found true pleasure out of Him any more than any person has been able to hear *with his eyes*, you will "*spend money for that which is not bread, and your labor for that which satisfieth not.*" Is not this madness? Forbear, then, vain man, to fight against God! Your folly has lasted sufficiently long already. Let a pious poet reason with you, who asks

"For the bright world of
Pure and boundless love,
What hast thou found? Alas, a narrow room!
Put out that light,
Restore thy soul its sight,
For better 't is to dwell in outward gloom,
Than by the vile body's eye
To rob the soul of its infinity."

If a man were about to emigrate to some far-off land, and to risk his whole fortune in the enterprise, he would assuredly listen to the words of experience. However bright the pictures of his fancy, however ardent his pantings after his imaginary elysium, he would certainly pause if *credible* men, returning from that new world of his hopes, should *uniformly* testify that although verdant as paradise and fruitful as Eden, a deadly malaria poisoned the atmosphere and made it a land of graves. Such testimony would surely cause a sane mind to change its purposes, and shun a danger so obvious and undeniable, "*for a wise man feareth and* DEPARTETH FROM EVIL; *but the fool rageth and* IS CONFIDENT."

Now I am able to offer you credible testimony from competent judges concerning the incapacity of this perishing world to give you the happiness it so falsely promises, and which you so credulously expect. Against your hopes lies the fact that, thus far, the world has not fulfilled its promises to you. Your present state is well described by one who tried your god faithfully, and said of his youth,

> "I was not happy, but I knew not then
> That happy I was never doom'd to be."

And this, if all past experience is not illusion, will be your sad conclusion if you continue the slave of the world. To feel convinced of this, study well the following testimonies:

KING SOLOMON tried an experiment with the world.

He wished to know if it contained aught that could confer real bliss. He had abundant means for his purposes. He tried the pleasures of wine, of feasting, of lust, of music, of building, of horticulture, of wealth, of power, of ambition, of greatness. In describing his attempt he says:

"WHATSOEVER *mine eyes desired I kept not from them. I withheld not my heart from any joy!"*

Thus he tried the world in all its forms. He brought all its resources to the test. Never, perhaps, has mortal man had equal opportunity to make such a trial of its power. What is his verdict? Hear it, child of pleasure! Ponder it well and deeply. "Behold!" he exclaims, after reviewing his experience, "BEHOLD, ALL WAS VANITY AND VEXATION OF SPIRIT!"

GELIMER was king of the Vandals, and was, for a time, a victorious, powerful sovereign. The pleasures of wealth, pomp, and ambition, flowed like streams into his heart. But they had no power to satisfy, for when led a captive, afterward, at the chariot wheels of his conqueror, Belisarius, through the streets of Constantinople, he too cried, "*Vanity of vanities! Vanity of vanities!*" An affecting testimony to the utter worthlessness of visible splendors and earthly good.

Behold also the magnanimous SALADIN, the noble hearted Saracen, an eastern sultan, whose bravery was only matched by that of the chivalrous Richard, England's lion-hearted king. After a life of successful wars, this mighty man lay on his couch pale and dying, surrounded by prince and paladin, peer and warrior. The expiring sultan bade them take his shroud, fasten it to his victorious banner-staff, and bid a herald carry it through the city streets, exclaiming as he went: "*This is all that is left, of all his greatness, to the mighty Saladin!*" What a bitter confession of the emptiness of worldly things was contained in this expressive command!

Hear still another. Let HORATIO NELSON speak. He entered upon his career a sickly boy, an almost unfriended coxswain in a British ship-of-war. He toiled hard and long for fame, honor, wealth. He gained them all. The pale-faced boy became an admiral, a viscount, a duke, a knight of various orders. He was the hero of a hundred fights. Whole nations feared him, while in his native land no man could excite such enthusiasm as thrilled the hearts of his countrymen when he appeared. He was literally covered with the glory of this world. Let him tell what the world did toward making him a happy man:

"I am now," he wrote, "I am now perfectly the great man: not a creature near me. *From my heart I wish myself the little man again!*

"THERE IS NO TRUE HAPPINESS IN THIS LIFE, and in my present state I could quit it with a smile. Believe me, my only wish is to sink with honor to the grave. I envy none but those of the estate of six feet by two!"

Listen again. The witness is hoary with age, and the wealthy owner of a magnificent palace. During his long life he was first a priest, then a bishop; next a merchant, then a statesman and diplomatist, a prince of the French empire, and the confidential adviser of that great warrior-king, Napoleon. His companions have been kings and warriors. His counsels have decided the fate of empires. His name is TALLEYRAND. Let him say how much happiness this world can yield its most successful votaries.

"Eighty-three years of life," he writes, "are now passed, filled with what anxieties! what agitations! what vanities! what troublous perplexities! And all this with no other result than great fatigue, and a *profound sentiment of discouragement with regard to the future, and of disgust for the past.*"

Now hear a gay sinner speak from the circles of private life. Writing to a friend he said: "There is not a blessing springs upon my path but mildew covers it; nor a flower that blooms there which does not wither and die. Although gray hairs have not silvered my head, yet my hopes are dead, and now in my prime I must, it is most likely, sink to my grave with an icy chillness round my heart. My life is steered by the chart of misery!"

Such is the voice of experience concerning the world. Its friends, too, are the speakers. I have purposely selected the verdicts of successful seekers after worldly joy. Had I given the opinion of spiritual Christians, you might have objected that they have to defend the consistency of their practice in forsaking the pleasures of this life, and are therefore interested witnesses. You cannot offer this reply to the parties before you. One of them, Solomon, was a Jew, Gelimer was a pagan, Saladin was a follower of Mohammed, Nelson a nominal Christian, Talleyrand was a Papist, and the gay sinner was a skeptic! But though differing so widely in their religious views and in their circumstances, they all testify to the utter insufficiency of the world to satisfy and make happy the immortal soul of man. Thus the sons of pleasure agree with experimental Christians, and with the Holy Scriptures, in teaching the vanity of mere earthly pleasures. They all sustain the poet who, in portraying the world, says:

> "The empty pageant rolls along;
> The giddy, inexperienced throng
> Pursue it with enchanted eyes;
> It passeth in swift march away;
> Still more and more its charms decay,
> Till the last gaudy color dies."

What *will* you—what *can* you reply to this overwhelming mass of evidence? You must stand speechless before it! You must be convinced by it! You must yield to its authority or be self-convicted of willful blindness. Let me persuade you to submit—to cast off the world: for even admitting it could give real bliss, and that all your expectations of attaining it will be realized, which is very uncertain, you will have, at best, but a small portion of its wealth or honor. Why then will you sell your present happiness and your soul for so uncertain and valueless a price? Study well this momentous problem: "WHAT SHALL IT PROFIT A MAN IF HE SHALL GAIN THE WHOLE WORLD AND LOSE HIS OWN SOUL? OR WHAT SHALL A MAN GIVE IN EXCHANGE FOR HIS SOUL?" Can you afford to make such a bargain? Will you sell your soul for a little sensual pleasure? Horrible bargain! Immortal blessedness sold for a world which, in its richest aspect, is vanity! Pause, beloved youth, ere you ratify such a fatal contract! Do not hide its true awfulness from your sight by saying you do not intend to cast off God and religion in following the pleasures of this world. The sacrifice of the Divine service, and of the soul, is inevitable if you will serve the world. "*Ye* CANNOT *serve God and mammon,*" and "*know ye not that the friendship of the world is enmity with God? Whosoever therefore will be a friend of the world is the enemy of God!*"

Choose, then, between this manifestly unsatisfying world and the salvation of your soul! The issue is plainly before you. Take this world and its short-lived vanities, and you shall lose the favor of God! heaven! your soul! Or, give up the world and God will give you himself, and save you with an everlasting life; for "*the fear of the Lord tendeth to life, and he who hath it shall abide satisfied; he shall not be visited with evil.*"

Bid your idol adieu, therefore, saying with Sir Henry Wotton:

"Farewell, ye gilded follies, pleasing troubles!
Farewell, ye honored rags, ye glorious bubbles!
Fame's but a hollow echo; gold, pure clay;
Honor, the darling but of one short day;
Beauty, the eye's idol, but a damask'd skin;
State, but a golden prison to live in,
And torture freeborn minds; embroidered trains,
Merely but pageants for proud swelling veins:
* * * * * *
Fame, honor, beauty, state, train, blood, and birth
Are but the fading blossoms of the earth."

CHAPTER II.

HOW TO ENJOY THIS LIFE.

THE Orientals relate a beautiful legend of their renowned calif, HAROUN AL RASCHID. He was riding one day with his train along a narrow street in Bagdad, when one of his camels stumbled. By its fall a casket of pearls was broken, and its precious contents scattered upon the ground. Nodding to his attendants, the calif gave them permission to gather the costly spoils for themselves. In an instant they rushed from his train to gather up the guerdon of their master—all but one stout, hideous-faced Ethiopian. "Moveless as the steed he reined," he still sat behind his lord. Surprised, the calif said:

"Tell me, good fellow, why you seek not your share of the pearls? What will you gain by thus lingering near to me?"

"My gain will be this, sire," replied the Ethiopian; "I shall know that I have faithfully guarded my king."

That noble reply won the calif's heart. Speaking of his faithful Ethiop to his friend, he said:

——— "No features fair
Nor comely mien are his;
Love is the beauty he doth wear,
And love his glory is."

This legend finely illustrates a difference between the Christian and the worldling. The former finds his good in the Creator himself, as the Ethiop found his gain in serving his king; the latter seeks his good in the "*creature*," as the calif's servants sought their gain in the scattered pearls. The former remembers, the latter forgets,

"That if thou not to Him aspire,
But to his gifts alone,
Not love, but covetous desire,
Has brought thee to his throne."

As a worldling, you, beloved youth, are falling into the sad mistake of the latter class. You are looking for happiness not in God, but in his gifts alone, in the scattered pearls of earth's broken casket. That this expectation must be quenched in the dead sea of disappointment I have, I trust, convinced you. Permit me now to unfold a truth which is probably new to you. Let me show you that the way to extract the utmost pleasure from the things of this life is not by a "studied indulgence of the appetites and passions," but by seeking your chief happiness in God.

Before entering further, however, on this subject, I must guard you against the dangerous idea that your personal enjoyment is the true end and aim of life. The poet, in his "Psalm of Life," teaches you better. He says:

> "Not enjoyment and not sorrow,
> Is our destined end or way;
> But to act, that each to-morrow
> Find us farther than to-day."

The poet is right. Your chief end is neither selfish joy nor selfish grief, but such earnest action — such a right use of your powers — as shall daily carry you farther from the selfish and the carnal, and nearer to the pure character of Him who is both the embodiment and the source of all real felicity. The result of that action will be the highest happiness, physical, mental, and spiritual, of which you are capable. If you will make it your object to attain the image of God, he will make it his care to promote your enjoyment. If his service is your delight, he will see to it that all things within you and without you contribute to your happiness. His whole nature, which is love, moves him to do this. Look backward along the far-stretching aisle of time. See the first pair as they came from his hands in Eden. So long as they made him the sole object of their loving service, he made everything tributary to their pleasure. Beauty filled their eyes, melody charmed their ears. Every movement of their limbs, every excitation of their senses, every gratification of their appetites, every agitation of their emotions, every exercise of their reasoning faculty, every thought of each other, every perception of the Creator, caused a fresh wave of delight to pass over their happy spirits. But when they turned their eyes from the Creator and set themselves to the work of seeking their own interests and pleasures in their own way, then, alas! happiness fled from Paradise and them. Then pain, and sorrow, and discord, and fear, were born into their hearts, and misery became the heir-loom of sinning mortals. Still God's desire for human happiness, like his loving nature, remained unchanged. But as man lost it by turning away from God as the supreme good, so he must recover it by turning to him again with devoted love and faithful service. Sought on selfish principles, and as a selfish end, happiness can never be found; but sought in God, it bubbles up within the soul "a well of water springing up unto eternal life."

You probably hold the opinion that to be pious you must so separate yourself from the world as to take no pleasure in anything but strictly religious exercises. You fancy that true piety prohibits you from enjoying any pleasure in earthly objects, pursuits, and associations; that it requires you to walk amid all the delights of this terrestrial life with elongated countenance, rigid muscles, and mournful step, like some grave mute at a funeral, or some half buried old monk of the middle ages, whose mystic creed taught him that he was in the high road to saintship because he could say:

> "I have torn up the roses from my garden
> And planted thorns instead; I have forged my griefs,
> And hugged the griefs I dared not forge; made earth
> A hell for heaven."

If you hold such views, you, like the monkish mystic, cherish a false opinion. True piety does not so war with your nature as to prohibit you from enjoying all the delight which springs from the *legit-*

imate exercises of your bodily senses and appetites, of your social affections, of your various emotions, and of your intellectual faculties. You may be eminently pious, and at the same time find pleasure in eating, drinking, hearing, seeing, feeling; in the transaction of business, and the accumulation of property; in cheerful, social intercourse with congenial minds; in intellectual pursuits, in the cultivation of the imagination and the esthetic tastes; in historic, philosophic, scientific studies. In brief, you may be a devoted Christian, and enjoy every pleasant sensation, emotion, and affection that can be called into activity, by external objects, *without violating the laws of your physical, moral, or intellectual nature.*

What piety *forbids* is not *use* but *excess.* It comes to all men, "teaching us that denying ungodliness and worldly lusts, we should live soberly, righteously, and godly in this present world." What piety *requires* is the *right use* of your senses, appetites, and emotions, and of those objects in the world which pleasurably excite them. The godly are "*they that* USE *this world as* NOT ABUSING *it.*" Even the dreaded *self-denial* which religion enjoins is not directed against the lawful use of things that are lawful, but against that powerful tendency to excessive self-indulgence which is the black brand on depraved human nature, and the source of those mighty conflicts between flesh and spirit, through which every earnest soul must pass that would enter the gate of eternal life. But as Orpheus with his lyre charmed the grim monarch of Hades into submission to his wishes, so piety in a good man's heart throws a spell of power over his appetites and passions, thereby bringing the carnal tendency of his nature into subjection to the law of righteousness. Let us view him in contrast with the worldling at this point.

The worldling yields to the cravings of his depraved nature, and indulges his sensations and emotions more than is either right or healthful; the pious mind conquers it, and rests satisfied with lawful and healthful pleasures. The worldling seeks sensible pleasures as the prime aim of his existence; the pious man accepts them as the seasoning of duty and a stimulant to its performance. The worldling "fulfills the lusts of the flesh," and plunges into "divers worldly lusts," such as gluttony, drunkenness, revelings, vain amusements, covetousness, and the like; the pious man "crucifies the flesh with its affections and lusts," keeps his "body under, and brings it into subjection" to the law of "temperance in all things." The worldling so indulges himself as to incur *guilt* in his pleasures; the pious man accepts such pleasure only as is consistent with the preservation of a pure conscience and a mind at peace with God. In a word, the worldling is the devoted slave of his appetites and passions; the pious man is their wise master and lord. Which, then, think you, is likely to derive the most pleasure from them through a lifetime? Their master or their slave?

To solve this problem you need only consider carefully what has been already stated, that the pious man keeps the laws of his physical, mental, and moral constitution in all his pleasures, while the worldling indulges himself without regard to those laws. Now, most assuredly, no man can, on the whole, extract more pleasure from his sensations and emotions by violating their laws than can be obtained from their lawful use. If he can, then God has so constituted men as to make disobedience more productive of happiness than obedience, which cannot be true. If he cannot, then a religious life, instead of depriving you of all sensible pleasures, is likely to afford you more enjoyment of earthly things than a sinful and worldly one, and to verify the saying of the Master: "*Seek first the kingdom of God and his righteousness, and all these things shall be added unto you.*" "He that keepeth the law, happy is he."

There is an old fable which will further illustrate the difference between the pious man and the worldling with respect to their enjoyment of this life. It describes a bee finding a jar of sweetmeats in a garden. Forsaking the flowers, it plunged into the jar of sweets and gave itself up to their enjoyment. Despising the tedious toil of its fellow-bees among the flowers, it clung to its abundance and eat to satiety. Cloyed at length, it sought to quit its pleasure-house and return to its hive. But its legs were buried in the sweets. Flapping its wings to escape, they too became immured in the luscious mire. Struggling still harder, it sunk deeper, and finally found death, where so lately it found nothing but delight.

That silly bee is a fitting type of the worldling, for like it he plunges into pleasures of appetite, sensation, or passion, and voraciously devours, while the good man cautiously sips. Like the bee, too, he may crowd more of enjoyment into a brief space of time than the good man can obtain from lawful moderation. But mark the result. The excess of his indulgence cloys his appetites; he is then afflicted with the nausea of satiety. Disgust deadens the raptures of desire. Exhaustion succeeds the excitement of passion. The vital forces having been too lavishly expended, become insufficient to impart healthful motion to the machinery of life, and its wheels begin to drag heavily along. The abused animal functions develop disease and feebleness, and he becomes incapable of enjoyment, and the victim of pain. Still his diseased imagination tyrannizes over his passions, his habits weave iron webs around him, and his imbecile will, unable to resist, permits him to be dragged, like a slave, into the embrace of pleasures which his cloyed heart loathes. Under this discipline of misery his mind and body soon break down. He lives on a wretched wreck of humanity, or stumbles prematurely into an unhonored grave.

Such is the worldling's pleasure. Now look again at the manner of the pious man's enjoyment of life, and its results. He places, as I have before shown, the law of God, as found in the Scriptures and in his own constitution, as a rein on the neck of his sensational and emotional nature, and thus restrains it from what is sinful. While he avoids excess, he extracts all lawful pleasure from every lawful object that can act upon his senses and emotions. Thus he enjoys life slowly; he gratifies, but does not cloy his appetites; hence he knows nothing of the nausea of satiety, the ennui of exhaustion, or the feebleness of abused powers. His vital forces remain vigorous and abundant; the currents of life flow healthfully along his veins; life is to him a daily benison. He enjoys his existence, and having thus carefully husbanded his vital forces until, by natural expenditure, they are exhausted, he finally passes from a peaceful death-bed into an honorable grave.*

* Commenting on the apostle's saying, "Godliness is profitable for the life that now is," ADAM CLARKE observes: "The man that fears, loves, and serves God, has God's blessing all through life. His religion saves him from all those excesses, both in action and passion, which sap the foundations of life, and render existence itself often a burden. The peace and love of God in the heart produce a serenity and calm which cause the lamp of life to burn clear, strong, and permanent. Evil and disorderly passions obscure and stifle the vital spark. Every truly religious man *extracts the uttermost good out of life itself*, and, through the Divine blessing, *gets the uttermost good that is in life;* and what is better than all, acquires a full preparation here below for an eternal

"How men would mock at Pleasure's shows,
Her golden promise, if they knew
What weary work she is to those
Who have no better work to do.

"Curved is the line of beauty,
Strait is the line of duty;
Walk by the last and thou shalt see
The other ever follow thee.

"O righteous doom, that they who make
Pleasures their only end,
Ordering their whole life for its sake,
Miss that whereto they trend:

"While they who bid stern duty lead,
Content to follow, they,
Of duty only taking heed,
Find pleasure by the way."

It is said of MAHMOUD, the great Mohammedan conqueror of India, that after his victory at Somnat he found a stupendous idol at the gates of its temple. "Destroy it!" cried the zealous warrior. "God is one; destroy this false idol!"

The Brahmins fell at his feet. "Spare our god Somnat," they pleaded; "we will give thee gold, pearls, and jewels of rarest luster."

life of glory above. Thus godliness has the promise of, and secures the blessings of both worlds."

"It must be destroyed," retorted the conqueror. "I would rather be remembered as the breaker than the seller of idols!" Having uttered these words,

"High he rear'd his battle-ax, and heavily came down the blow;
Reel'd the abominable image, broken, bursten, to and fro—
From its shatter'd sides revealing pearls, and diamonds, showers of gold;
More than all that proffer'd ransom, more than all a hundred-fold."

As with Mahmoud and the idol, so must it be with thee and the world, my reader. To enjoy it you must smite it. To win the wealth of pleasure it contains you must dethrone it, die to it, despise it, conquer it. You must abandon its gay haunts and refuse to touch its sinful amusements; you must shun the ball-room, the theater, the opera-house, the gambling saloon, with every haunt of folly; you must detach your affections from its wealth, its honors, its fashions. But in doing all this, you sacrifice no real pleasure; you do not diminish the degree of enjoyment which life can extract from the earthly; on the contrary, He, to gain whose love you flee these sinful things, will compel the world to pour its pearls into your lap—to bring you as much of its innocent pleasures as may be consistent with your highest interests—

your eternal happiness—to yield you more pure pleasure than godless worldling ever knew. Smite, then! Smite thy idol world to the dust. Seek its sinful pleasures no longer:

> "Fond youth, give o'er,
> And vex thy soul no more
> In seeking what were better far unfound;
> Alas! thy gains
> Are only present pains
> To gather scorpions for a future wound."

But gather up your soul's affections; bind yourself with them to the cross of Jesus, and consecrate your noble nature to Him whose service is freedom, whose laws are paths of happiness, and at whose right hand there are "pleasures for evermore." Thus shall your glad heart be

> "A hidden fountain fed from unseen springs
> From the glad-making river of our God."

CHAPTER III.

THE SOCIAL HAZARDS OF A SINFUL LIFE.

A LITTLE more than a century ago a young man named WILLIAM DODD graduated with eclat at Cambridge University, England. Being the son of a clergyman he had enjoyed the benefits of early religious training. Having the advantages of a fine person, a superior mind, a thorough education, and good family connections, his life-prospects were as bright and promising as those of any young man in his class. Who could have predicted that such a fair beginning would be succeeded by an ignoble end? Yet so it was.

For a time this young man's path was sunlit, and his hopes bloomed out into beautiful successes. Having entered the ministry he soon became singularly popular. His fine physique, charming voice, elegant manners, and eloquent utterances, led admiring thousands to throng his church. Nobles, wits, and highborn ladies heard him with delight, and filled his ears with their flatteries. Preferments followed in the wake of popularity. Lectureships, college titles, a prebend's stall, a royal chaplaincy, a vicarage, and the tutorship of the young Earl of Chesterfield, were given him. The highest honors of his exalted profession hung like ripening fruit within his grasp.

Alas for this favored child of Providence! His priestly robes concealed a worldling's heart. An insane passion for the society of the wealthy, the titled, and the nobly born, burned like a consuming flame in his breast. He yielded himself to its impulses, and it beguiled him into a style of living, the expenses of which preyed like locusts on his income, and made him poor in the midst of plenty. Reason pleaded and conscience protested against this passion in vain. It was his Calypso. Syren-like, it fascinated him, and drew him farther and farther from the line of duty, until it bound him in heavy chains of impracticable debts.

Then came a hopeless struggle for freedom, which ended only with his utter ruin. Still listening to the voices of his passion, he tried to break his chains with the hammer of crime. First he sought to win the gift of a rich rectory by offering a bribe to the lady of the lord chancellor. He was repelled with merited scorn, and scourged by the popular tongue into disgraceful privacy.

Would that this stern rebuke had been heeded. But it was not. His passion lived. His debts were still unpaid. Then his evil genius triumphed, and in a sad, sad moment, he forged a bond for over twenty thousand dollars! The deed was discovered. He was tried, convicted, sentenced to death, and twenty-six years after his graduation at Cambridge, the eloquent and popular William Dodd, D.D., LL.D., expiated his crime on the felon's scaffold.

In this unhappy man behold the type of a class of persons which may be counted by thousands and tens of thousands, as they throng the highways and byways of society. They may be found in prisons, in alms-houses, in cellars and garrets, in dens of shame, in haunts of poverty, and in the hiding-places of crime. Like Dr. Dodd, multitudes of them once stood on no despicable moral and social height. The probabilities of a reputable, virtuous, and prosperous career, were in their case fully equal to those of the average of unrenewed men and women. The great social wheel which, in its endless revolutions, is continually reversing the positions of men, seemed more likely to carry them up than to cast them down to the dust. But, like Dr. Dodd, instead of seeking their supreme good in their Creator, they sought it in the creature. As he chose to feed on the foam of human praise, and to regard the gay circles of fashionable life as his soul's heaven, so they elected to feed on the ashes of some perishable delight and to find their paradise in the present. Hence, like the unhappy Dodd, having separated themselves from their Creator, they became the victims of their own lusts. Their own desires growing imperious, led them with an imperial arm down to the depths of sorrow, poverty, shame, or crime.

"What has all this to do with me?" inquires my reader. You might as wisely ask what the soldier has to do with the clarion's voice? What the mariner with the bell which utters its solemn warning as it sways over the sunken rock? Has not the history of Dr. Dodd, and the class of ruined ones he represents, a clarion's voice, a bell's note of alarm for you? Have you not entered the fatal door by which they passed into the house of shame and sorrow? Are you not, like them, seeking your supreme good, not in God, but in the creature? Are you not then liable to share their destiny? I speak not now of the final loss of your immortal soul, but of the liabilities of your life this side the tomb. My question is this: you have chosen the world to be your chief good—your God; are you not, therefore, in danger of falling into the same category with Dr. Dodd and his class, and of ending your life in shame, sorrow, poverty, or crime? Painfully as the thought may strike you, I affirm that such a destiny threatens you. It yawns, like a fearful chasm, in the path you have entered. I do not assert that you will certainly stumble into it if you refuse to become a Christian, because the restraining grace of God, and the grace of favoring circumstances, may save you. What I affirm is, your *liability* as a worldling to pluck down ruin upon your head, and make a sad, sad failure of your life on this side the grave.

You do not believe it? I presume not. Young sinners are not easily convinced, because they do not *see* their danger. They walk on enchanted ground. They are in the "way which," as the All-knowing One describes it, "seemeth right unto a man," though at the "end thereof are the ways of death." Would that I could disenchant thee, my beloved reader!

When Sisera, the Canaanite warrior, fled defeated before the sword of Barak, he sought a hiding-place in the tent of JAEL. That subtle lady welcomed him with smiles, and bade him rest in quiet under her protection. Confiding in her friendly professions, the weary soldier "asked water and she gave him milk; she brought forth butter in a lordly dish." He ate and drank, and then sought refuge from the pangs of defeat in sleep. Then Jael "put her hand to the nail and her right hand to the workman's hammer; and with the hammer she smote Sisera, she smote off his head, when she had pierced and stricken through his temples."

Alas, poor Sisera! The smile of Jael was more fatal to him than the steel of his foes: and alas for thee too, young worldling! for although the goddess of sinful pleasure, like Jael, smiles on thee and brings thee "butter in a lordly dish," yet she carries the hammer and the nail beneath her vestments; and when thy conscience is fast locked in the slumber of folly, she will smite thee a deadly blow, which will leave thee rolling in the dust of shame, or plunge thee into the gloom of death.

It is this deceptiveness, this concealment of the skeleton beneath a beautiful mask, which makes a life of devotion to sinful pleasure so perilous. If the word poison was graven on its cup, if the draught it offers was bitter to the taste, there would be less of danger. But it is not so. The false goddess mixes a charmed draught in a chased cup. Her poison is a slow one too. It does its work so gradually, that he who drinks it finds it difficult to believe there is evil in the draught at all. Did Dr. Dodd dream of his fate, think you, when he first quaffed the wine of flattery? He smacked his lips over it with delight; he was mentally intoxicated; but he dreamed not that the folly which led him to prefer the praise of men to the praises of God, was the first step toward social shame. Yet so it was, for

> "Adulation is the death of virtue;
> Who flatters, is of all mankind the lowest,
> Save he who courts flattery."

Dr. Dodd, as we have seen, was foolish enough first to love and then to court the flattery of the great. That folly led him into habits of extravagance. Those habits plunged him into debt. His debts goaded him until, becoming distrustful of his friends and reckless of consequences, he plunged into crime and perished on the scaffold.

Folly, then, was the first step in his downward career. And is not *folly* the first step in the descent of all who sink into the pit of social shame? Is it not the first link in the chain which binds every demoralized and degraded man and woman now groaning in the mire of infamy? Did ever drunkard, gambler, debauchee, forger, political profligate, or defalcator, plunge from the pure heights of virtuous life into the slough of gross and daring sin at a single leap? Never! Never! Trace the fall of all such persons back to its source and you will find some folly—perhaps a venial one only—at the beginning. Vanity, seeking gratification in the admiration of men, led that poor poverty-stricken mother into the *folly* of the ill-advised marriage which dragged her down to her present cheerless lot. The same weakness also led that pitiable creature, whose presence now pollutes the street, into the *folly* of extravagant dress, of seeking gay society, or of listening to the voices of the flatterer, until she was beguiled of woman's most precious jewel. The *folly* of aping his superiors in wealth led that forger into the financial embarrassments which resulted in crime. The *folly* of making haste to be rich led that defalcator to appropriate the property of others to his own uses. The *folly* of yielding to the fascination of a gay associate seduced that gambler and that drunkard to frequent the "hells" in which their moral ruin was consummated. In short, study the life of any degraded man or woman, either of the past or present, and you will find the germ of their corruption concealed in some sinful or venial folly of their early lives. Every such life is but the fulfillment of the Divine prediction: "*In the greatness of his* FOLLY *he shall go astray!*"

Let me strengthen my argument by another fact. There is in the nature of every human being some weak moral point at which he is peculiarly accessible. In other words, there is in all some marked constitutional tendency which seeks its development in some one or more of those specific follies which have resulted in the ruin of all the socially fallen. One, for instance, is inclined to pride, another to vanity, a third is strongly predisposed to covetousness, a fourth to ambition, a fifth to amativeness, and a sixth to violent outbursts of anger. Others, again, have a tendency to gluttony, indolence, obstinate self-will, or to falsehood. In every breast the currents of nature set strongly in one or more of these evil directions. Even St. Paul, in his regenerated state, was so conscious of the presence of an "easily besetting" or constitutional sin, that he required all the energy of his great will, aided by the grace of God, to struggle successfully with it. Hear his notable confession: "I keep under my body and bring it into subjection, lest that by any means, when I have preached to others, I myself should be a castaway."

I assume, therefore, dear young reader, that there are, in *your nature*, some *strong tendencies to particular forms of sin*. I know not what they are. You may be proud, vain, covetous, lustful, passionate, or self-willed. But be your tendencies what they may, they are active, and ever prompting you to the perpetration of one or more of those specific follies which have led thousands, yea, tens of thousands, into shame and sorrow; for

"As eagerly the barr'd up bird will beat
And beak against his wiry dome,
Till the blood tinge his plumage, so the heat
Of your impellèd soul will through your bosom burn."

Are you not, therefore, in danger of sharing their fate? Are not your natural tendencies, if unchecked by religious restraint, and cherished by your devotion to the earthly, liable, at least, to forge a chain of follies with which to bind you at length to the pillory of shame? Is it not clear to your own consciousness, that as you possess the precise tendencies which have led millions into such follies, you too are liable to be found in the same category with the morally ruined and the socially fallen?

"Self-love is the greatest of all flatterers." It doubtless whispers words of safety in your ears, assuring you that however other irreligious youths may have rushed on ruin, *you* are safe. Well, perhaps you are. True, you are advancing along a road bristling with the steel of countless foes, yet it may be you carry a charmed life, or you wear linked armor, so nicely fitted, and of such rare proof that no fiery arrow or stout broadsword of temptation can pierce or break it. It may be so and it may not; but since the peril is great, and the consequences of a mistake inconceivably fearful, would it not be well for you to look at your means of defense? Suffer me, therefore, to ask you, On what do you rely for moral safety in this path of worldly pleasure which you have chosen?

Let me portray a scene from history. A beautiful valley, situated between two small hills, was made a battle-field by two armies, whose white tents and fluttering pennons crowned the opposite heights. In the middle of the vale there strode a colossal warrior, full nine feet in height, and with a frame duly proportioned. He was cased from head to foot with armor of brass. In his hand he bore a spear. With vaunting words he dared the bravest of his foes to meet him in single combat.

Responding to his challenge, there came a slender youth in shepherd's garb. He was beautiful though small in stature. His step was light, his form erect. He wore no armor, he carried neither sword nor spear. His only weapon was a sling.

His gigantic adversary sneered bitterly at his weakness, and thought to make him an easy prey. But the stripling, stepping boldly forward, said: "I come to thee in the name of the Lord of Hosts," and slung a stone which, striking the giant's forehead, caused him to fall on his face a dead man.

Now, my dear young reader, if you were advancing, like David, toward the gigantic dangers which stand in your path, *with the "Lord of Hosts" to help you*, I would not cherish a particle of anxiety in your behalf. But alas! alas! that Divine aid, which is the only help sufficient to secure any man the victory in the battle of life, you deliberately refuse. Like David, you are obviously inferior to your foes, but you reject David's helper; while, with none of Goliah's might, you cherish his self-sufficiency, and are rushing to the conflicts of life, trusting in your own puny strength. Let us see wherein your power to overcome lies.

You have, I presume, a well-educated conscience, which, it must be admitted, is a powerful guardian. Millions have been saved from ruin by giving heed to its monitions. Yours would restrain you from ruinous follies, if you would but enthrone it in your heart, and do it homage as to the Viceroy of heaven. But this you will not do, as your rejection of God as your supreme good plainly shows. Just here then lies your danger. You have already dethroned your conscience. Its voice has little or no authority over your desires and passions. Your enslaved will forswore allegiance to it, when it yielded itself to the sway of your worldly lusts. With what propriety, then, can you depend on this ill-treated faculty to restrain you in the hour of fierce temptation? When your love of creature good shall have placed you in the pillory of folly, when some Circe shall display her meretricious charms and stir your passions with her songs; when your adored and worshiped world shall tempt you to the embraces of some hitherto unenjoyed, but wicked, perhaps profitable delight, what aid will your poor, abused, tongue-tied, narcotized conscience be able to afford? You will be on the brink of destruction. Like the ancient Romans when they had banished their noblest and only chief capable of saving them from their terrible enemies, the Gauls, you will be counted happy if, like them, you can recall your deliverer to its seat of authority in season to save yourself from ruin. Is it prudent to run the fearful risk?

Many persons there are whose pride of character, or, as they would improperly name it, self-respect, restrains them from doing mean, degrading, or criminal actions. They partake of the spirit of a Scotchman named DOUGLAS. This fool-hardy hero commanded a British ship-of-war, and being stationed in the river Medway to resist the advance of a Dutch fleet, he was ordered to defend his ship to the last extremity, but in no case to retire from his position. Bravely he fought, until his ship took fire; but even then, when the most rigorous authority could require no more, he refused to quit her deck, and perished in the flames, exclaiming, "A Douglas was never known to quit his post without orders!"

In this scion of a noble house pride of character was stronger than the love of life. In some minds it is sufficiently strong to restrain them from degrading pleasures and from dishonorable actions *under ordinary circumstances.* Possibly it is so in you, my reader. Your pride takes fire at the bare suggestion that you will ever become the victim of those vices which degrade and plunge men and women into shame. Panoplied in pride of character, you feel like an unlucky hero, named ANXUR, in Virgil's Eneis:

> "Anxur had boasted much of magic charms,
> And thought he wore impenetrable arms;"

but when he met the Trojan hero in the strife of battle, his boasted arms were bootless to protect him. Eneas saw him, and

> "At Anxur's shield he drove, and at one blow
> Both shield and arm to ground together go."

And thus it may be with your pride of character. Under ordinary temptations it may preserve you; but it is the misfortune of most who elect the world to be their god, that circumstances are created by their sinful pursuits which bring them into conflict with overwhelming temptations, before which they fall as swiftly and easily as did the boastful Anxur beneath the sword of stern Eneas.

Take for illustration the sad example of that wretched traitor, BENEDICT ARNOLD. Favored by nature with brilliant military talents, and by gentle providences with favorable opportunities, he found himself in the prime of life a patriot general, a popular and honored soldier, the husband of a beautiful wife, and the possessor of an income ample enough to satisfy every reasonable want.

But Benedict Arnold had long cherished an inordinate self-esteem. Prosperity stimulated its growth, and caused it to become his evil genius. Pride, vanity, and ambition, took entire possession of his soul. To maintain a splendid establishment he sacrificed his property. And just then, when his pride of character ought to have held him back from wrong, he was tempted to dishonest peculations in his disbursements of the public money. Discovered and reprimanded by order of Congress, his now gloomy soul gave birth to purposes of revenge. Pride of character controlled him no more, for avarice and revenge tore it up by the roots. Then he chose a traitor's destiny, and sought, as you know, to sell his country for paltry place and paltrier gold. His plans were confounded. He fled, and gained a general's commission in the British army, and abundant gold; yet with these gains there came a new-born nation's hatred and the scorn of an indignant world. Never did mortal man start in life with greater pride of character, and never did mortal man go to his grave with more of shame and infamy than this same Benedict Arnold, the traitor.

Such is the weakness of pride of character, even in an extraordinary man, when strong temptations, like armed men, enter his soul. How then, my dear young reader, can you rely with anything like confidence on your pride of character for protection against those mighty assaults on the passions to which a worldly life will assuredly expose you?

But you feel no inclination to perpetrate those acts which lead to disgrace? Probably you do not. Your master passion is not yet fully grown. Your hour of conflict is not yet. Does that prove it will never come? May the spark be despised because it is not yet a devouring flame? Look into your heart not for a present inclination to dangerous vices, but for the presence of those tendencies which lead men into the circumstances which beget uncontrollable lusts.

A gentleman in India once reared a tiger's cub. His kindness seemed to eradicate the ferocity of its nature, and it grew up docile as a pet dog. One day its owner, being alone with it in his library, caressed it and gave it his hand to lick. The rough tongue of the animal grazed his skin and gave it its first taste of blood. Then its ferocious nature awaked. Fury gleamed from its eye, and couching itself it made ready to spring upon its master. Fortunately the gentleman had a loaded pistol on his table, and saved his life by shooting his former pet.

Let this fact illustrate a valuable truth. Let the sleeping ferocity of the tiger, waked by the taste of blood, stand for a figure of that slumbering passion in your breast which needs but the taste of strong temptation to rise into a terrible life, and to break over all the feeble defenses which a maltreated conscience, and pride of character, may have built up in your soul to protect its virtue. One moment of triumphant passion may suffice to undo the work of half a lifetime. And *you*, have *you* not this tiger in your breast?

But you have established moral habits, and you rely on their protection, perhaps. Well, I congratulate you heartily. Good moral habits are very desirable guardians, and if they have been formed in obedience to the conscience and the religious affections, they are as powerful to protect as the angelic forces which guarded Elisha on the hill of Dothan.

Search, then, beloved reader, for the origin of these boasted moral habits. Scrutinize them narrowly. They may be little better than spies and traitors in the uniform of loyalists. Seize them therefore. Search them. Challenge them as to whence they came and whither they tend! See if the best of them are not merely negative virtues after all—that is, you habitually avoid certain forms of sin because you have no natural inclination for them. For example, you are not a miser, because your nature is not avaricious; you are not a spendthrift, because your nature inclines you to save rather than to waste; you are not given to noise and quarrel, because your nature inclines you to quiet and peace. These, with kindred habits, hardly merit the name of virtues, because they require no effort—no earnest willing. They are little else than the passive outgrowths of your mental constitution, just as docility, fidelity, peacefulness are the results of organization in some of the inferior animals.

Search, again, and see if others of your habits do not proceed from your education, your life associations, your pride of character, your self-esteem, your love of approbation, your fear of obloquy or physical suffering, or some other merely selfish motive? Look closely and I think you will discover SELF to be the sovereign to whom these boasted moral habits do homage. The bare fact that you choose the world, instead of the Creator, to be your supreme good, demonstrates that self is king in your soul, and therefore lord over your habits. You do not, because you cannot, serve both God and mammon. Confessedly, God does not reign in you, and therefore SELFISHNESS must.

But are *selfish* habits reliable protectors in those conflicts with the passions to which you stand exposed? Remember, these passions make their appeal to that very selfishness from which your present habits have sprung. Self-will, self-interest, self-pleasing—not respect for God and duty—have made you what you are. What may not happen, therefore, if, in the exigencies of your future life, the now half-awakened passion of acquisitiveness, or ambition, or amativeness, should plead with self-interest or self-pleasing for dangerous and unlawful indulgences. Would your old habits be likely to resist the pleadings of their own parents, think you? They might; and so might a fence of rushes check the march of the awful avalanche; yet who would feel like building his house beside such a fence, with the snow masses trembling above him, ready to fall under the tread of a passing chamois?

It cannot be; selfish habits cannot protect you from the assaults of temptations which appeal to the very selfishness which gave them birth. On the contrary, such habits serve to betray your soul by preparing it for defeat in the hour of trial. What are these habits but repeated acts of fealty to the dominant principle of selfishness? What are they but the jailers of your worldly mind, binding its will with chains of steel to the throne of selfishness, and keeping vigilant watch and ward over it, lest it should flee its bondage, and achieve its freedom by submission to God and duty?

These questions must be answered in the affirmative. What then? Why it follows that you have already parted with your freedom to resist the solicitations of selfish passions. Your moral habits, of which you boast, are but the chains with which the selfish or carnal mind has bound you. Like Paul's unrenewed man, you are carnal, sold under sin. Let me illustrate your condition.

There is an ancient tale which tells of a wandering princess who found an asylum in a deserted palace. Pleased with its quiet, she sought rest from her fatigues in its deserted chambers, and made it her temporary home. Day after day she walked up and down its grand old halls, and wandered through its vast apartments, thinking herself free and alone. Its gates stood open as when she entered, only a spider had stretched his fine, light, almost invisible web across the portals. This is a feeble obstacle, and the princess feels no doubt of her power to brush it aside with her delicate fingers when she is ready to resume her journey.

At length she resolves to quit the place. She

raises the web very easily, but there is a second one behind. She pushes this aside, when a third bars her way. This is lifted, but there is a fourth, a fifth, a sixth! Boldly she pushes them aside, but still web succeeds web. Her strength is put forth until she is ready to drop with fatigue. But her heart is bold and she struggles still. Vain struggles! There is no end to these obstructing webs. They are fine, light, but mighty in their self-renewing strength. They exhaust both her power and her courage. She gives up the contest. Her hands fall listlessly by her side. The princess is a prisoner!

Poor young princess! Poor young worldling! Like her, you move with pleasure in a palace of beauty and delight, cherishing the fancy that you are free to go or to remain, to drink deeply or lightly of the wine of selfish indulgences, or to abstain altogether if you so will. And like her you see not how selfish habits are weaving webs in your path, nor how one sinful habit leads to another, until the gorgeous world of your sinful choice will become your Bastile, from which you will find no egress save by the low gateway of faith in Christ, or by the "sorrow of the world," and eternal death.

Do you doubt this view of your liberty? Test it, then, by an experiment on yourself. Free yourself from the bands of your favorite pleasures. Break away from your chosen haunts and from your elect companions. Abandon the god of this world, and attempt to take your first steps in the path of religious duty, which is the way of true virtue! Try to do these things with all the moral might of your unassisted nature, and see if you do not find yourself the slave of your own selfish lusts—see if with Paul's unregenerate man you are not soon led to cry out, "How to perform that which is good I find not," and if, persisting in the trial, you do not at length groan out your despair by crying, "O wretched man that I am! who shall deliver me from the body of this death?"

Trust not, therefore, for security against the great and terrible liabilities of your earthly career, to your moral habits, your pride of character, or your faithful but much maltreated conscience. They are not reliable guardians over your safety. They cannot grapple with such foes to your life-success as crowd the highways of the gay world you have chosen to serve. If you will trust to them you will, in all probability, be left to fall into some folly which will be the evil genius of your life. Your vanity, or pride, or love of power, or lust of gain, your social affections, or your quick imperious temper, your envy, malice, or revenge, your dread of poverty, your fear of ridicule, or some other selfish desire, passion, or propensity, will drag you down from the serene heights of peaceful innocence into the gloomy valleys of mental wretchedness, and, it may be, into the still gloomier depths of poverty, shame, and possibly of crime.

Pause, then, beloved young worldling, in your gay career. Listen to the warning voice of him who, knowing the path you tread, says of it: "*There is a way which seemeth right unto a man, but the end thereof are the ways of death.*" Consider also these lines of old Francis Quarles:

> " O what a crocodilian world is this,
> Composed of treacheries and ensnaring wiles!
> She clothes destruction in a formal kiss,
> And lodges death in her deceitful smiles;
> She hugs the soul she hates; and then does prove
> The veriest tyrant where she vows to love;
> And is a serpent most when most she seems a dove."

CHAPTER IV.

LINKED ARMOR FOR TEMPTED YOUNG SOULS.

NAPOLEON, that most daring of warriors, rarely ventured on the hazardous measures which characterized his campaigns, without preparing beforehand for every conceivable emergency. His most brilliant victories were preceded by the most studiously prepared precautions against the possibilities of defeat. This habit gave him and his army confidence in the hour of peril. His failure to abide by it in his Russian campaign led to the disasters of his retreat from Moscow. Had he begun his splendid military career with such neglect, it would have been broken off at its beginning. He would have found his Waterloo at Austerlitz.

Let me persuade you, my dear reader, to adopt his habit of precaution in the great campaign of life. You have seen that, in common with all your species, your nature has tendencies to acts which may involve you in social shame, and bring you to a disreputable grave. You have also seen how totally unreliable your present means of protection are. Seeing then that you are exposed to so serious a danger, and are so unprepared to meet it, you cannot be without a strong desire to know on what you may rely for victory in this inevitable battle. To suppose the contrary would be to offër an insult to your reason, because it would presume you to be indifferent to one of your most important life interests. *You* are not thus indifferent. You have a desire to avoid the ruin of your earthly well-being. Having made a prosperous entrance upon the stage of life, you would like to make your exit from it at last without dishonor.

Suffer me, therefore, to point you to the religion of Jesus Christ as the only reliable means of self-conquest, and of victory over those tempters of the passions, desires, and affections which seek your ruin. Hear what the Holy Spirit saith to you on this subject: "*Whatsoever is born of God overcometh the world. Who is he that overcometh the world, but he that believeth that Jesus is the Son of God? He that is begotten of God keepeth himself, and that wicked one toucheth him not.*"

These are the words of Divine wisdom. They teach you that a renewed heart sustained by faith in Christ, and that only, can secure you that victory over yourself and the world which, as I have shown, is the condition of your moral safety. Let me now show you how a renewed heart fits its possessor for successful conflict in the battle of life. Two facts, taken from the lives of two holy men, will bring out one of its methods.

Three hundred years ago a weaver's apprentice, named William Hunter, was cast into prison by the ferocious Bishop Bonner for reading the Bible and professing his faith in its doctrines. After being confined in the stocks and loaded with chains, through nine weary months of life, in a wretched dungeon, the youth was carried before the bishop.

"If you recant," said that mitered monster, "I will give you forty pounds and set you up in business."

The youth modestly but firmly declined the offer.

"I will make you steward of my own house," added Bonner, putting all the gentleness of which his brutal nature was capable into his voice and manner.

"But, my lord," replied the lad, "if you cannot

persuade my *conscience* by Scripture, I cannot find it in my heart to turn from God for the love of the world; for I count all worldly things but loss in comparison with the love of Christ."

The bishop was enraged: "Will neither threats nor promises avail?" he cried. "Then away with him to the fire!"

And to the fire he went, firmly, fearlessly, joyfully. "I am not afraid!" he shouted from amid the flames, and his noble spirit ascended to heaven.

My second fact relates to GORDON HALL. God called him to the work of missions, and he went to the East Indies. After a time his influence with the natives became powerful. This, with his other qualifications, made his services desirable to the East India Company. They offered him thirteen thousand dollars a year if he would quit his missionary work and enter their service. He refused. They then offered him fifty dollars a week for occasional aid. This also he declined in these noble words:

"No money can tempt me to relinquish my work!"

In these two facts you cannot fail to see the more than regal sway which *conscience* maintained over the souls of these good men. With the martyr's fire on one side, and the favor of a rich and powerful bishop on the other, young Hunter's *conscience* made him superior both to the fear of death and the attractions of gold. It bound him to the post of duty, albeit it was in the midst of flames.

So also in the case of Gordon Hall. A high and honorable office tempted his ambition; a life of light labor pleaded with his love of ease; mammon appealed to his love of gain. All these combined to induce him to quit the post of duty, which was set in the midst of toils and poverty. But his *conscience* bound him firmly to the right, and kept him from forsaking his Master's work.

Hence, in these examples you see an effect of the regenerated life. It quickens, illuminates, and enthrones the conscience, so that it is not that narcotized, abused, and enfeebled thing which it is in the unregenerate breast. There, as I have shown, it is a slumbering slave. In the renewed man it is an active sovereign. Christ has set it free from the thrall of the passions, throned it, crowned it, and endowed it as his viceroy with authority over the will and the affections. The illumination of the Spirit has given it quick and far-reaching perceptions of right and wrong. It is, therefore, a POWER in the converted soul, and can be relied upon in the fierce conflicts which await every man in the great battle-fields of life. Of a man in whom conscience is thus enthroned it may with propriety be said:

> "Rather hope to shake
> The mountain-pine, whose twisting fibers clasp
> The earth, deep-rooted! Rather hope to shake
> The Scythian Taurus from his central base,"

than to allure him into the forbidden paths which lead to ruin.

It has been finely said by a poet that

> "Each man should think himself an *act* of God,
> His mind a thought, his life a breath of God.
> And each should try, by great thoughts and good deeds,
> To show the most of heaven he hath in him."

Another poet, writing of the human soul, has said:

> "Immortal! what can strike the sense so strong
> As this the soul? It thunders to the thought,
> Reason amazes, gratitude o'erwhelms.
> Roused at the sound, the exulting soul ascends
> And breathes her native air, an air that feeds
> Ambitions high, and fans ethereal fires,
> Quick kindles all that is divine within us,
> Nor leaves one loitering thought beneath the stars."

Such are the thoughts which dwell in the hearts of pious men. They constantly view themselves as the offspring, the redeemed, the beloved of God. They think much of their immortal nature and destiny. They regard themselves as the "sons of God," as having the divine Jesus for their "elder brother," and as being "heirs of God and joint heirs with Jesus Christ." These great thoughts are habitually present with them, refreshing them, and acting with indescribable power upon the growth of their characters.

Can you not readily perceive, my dear reader, how such thoughts as these tend to beget a degree of self-respect which cannot fail to act as a restraining power in the soul? Will he, think you, who feels such a consciousness of the essential value of his nature, of his infinitely exalted relationships, and of his noble destiny, be likely to cast himself and his prospects away for such momentary pleasures and perishable possessions as make their appeal to the senses, appetites, and passions of men? Will he not rather repel such temptations with such questions as these: "Shall I throw this immortal soul away for a mortal joy? Shall I, for a moment of forbidden delight, dash the cup, filled with the pure nectar of eternal bliss, from my lips? Shall I, who have been bought by the precious blood of Jesus Christ, and who am a child of God, degrade myself to the level of beasts and wicked angels?"

Now as a sinner you cannot be the possessor of this self-respect either in kind or degree. You may have pride of character, self-esteem, love of approbation, and up to a certain point they may afford you a doubtful protection; but, unless you become pious, that powerful self-respect which springs from deep convictions of the value of your spiritual nature cannot be yours. Why it cannot is clear as a sunbeam. For, so long as you are purposed to remain a sinner, you will necessarily put all thoughts of your immortal nature and destiny as far away from your mind as possible. Your human relations, your present pleasures, your earthly affairs, are and will be the chosen themes of your thoughts, to the exclusion of those ideas which are seeds of true, saving self-respect. Thus, you perceive, the regenerate life gives its possessor an ennobling self-respect, which, while it exalts his character, becomes as linked armor to his soul in its battles with those things which first demoralize and then destroy.

Love to Christ is also a principle of power in the heart of a pious youth. Let me illustrate its operation.

Two boys, the one a peasant, the other the son of a British nobleman, were tenderly attached to each other. The youthful lord was consumptive. As his disease progressed he grew feeble, until he was unable to leave his bed. Daily his peasant friend stood beside his bed and cheered him with many a smile and pleasant word. One day the sick boy wished for some blue-bells fresh from the hillside on which the boys had so often rambled in company. Eager to gratify his dying friend, the peasant boy hasted away, climbed the hill-top, and plucked the brightest and best of the flowers. At length he saw a beauty growing far out on the edge of a deep ravine. Thinking only of giving pleasure to his friend, regardless of himself, he stepped to pluck the coveted flower, when lo, he grew dizzy and fell ten fathoms deep into the gulf below! There his friends found him lifeless, with the wild flowers firmly clutched in his dead hand! The dear boy had fallen a sacrifice to the love he bore to his sick friend!

In this simple incident you see how affection moved

that peasant boy to forget himself through strong desire to give pleasure to his friend. First, it led him to deny himself his usual out-door sports and confine himself to the sick-chamber of his companion. Next, it gave wings to his feet when his sick playmate desired the wild flowers. And then it quieted every fear of danger on the edge of the ravine, and led him even into the very mouth of death. Was not his love a principle of power?

It is even so with that love for Christ which is begotten in the heart of him who is regenerated. His love for Christ makes it easy for him to do what pleases the Master, and to avoid what displeases him. When the breath of temptation stirs the seas of inborn passion to a state of tumult, when favoring opportunity invites unlawful indulgences, and when all that is attractive in the pomp of life, in the baits of ambition, and in the enticements of gain, pleads with his selfishness until his WILL trembles like a magnetic needle, then his love for Christ becomes a principle of power within him. He thinks of his Saviour, and his desire to please him grows so strong as to overpower all other desires. As the beloved image rises before his vision, his heart glows with the warmth of renewed affection, his will waxes strong, and he snaps the bands of temptation as Samson broke the cords with which the craft of Delilah had bound him. Animated by this love, he can do or not do, suffer or endure what would be impossible to his nature without it. If his love is deep and strong he can say with the holy RUTHERFORD: "If it were possible that heaven, yea, ten heavens, were laid in the balance with Christ, I would think the smell of his breath above them all." With such a love, he can say with faithful PAUL: "I can do all things through Christ that strengtheneth me."

> "Ah, how skillful grows the hand
> That obeyeth love's command!
> It is the *heart* and not the brain,
> That to the highest doth attain;
> And he that followeth love's behest
> Far exceedeth all the rest."

Thus you see, dear young friend, that the possession of piety would endow you with a principle of power, of which it may be said, as David remarked of the sword of Goliah, "there is none like it," except, indeed, that direct help from God himself which always assists the disciples of Christ when engaged in their conflicts with evil and the evil one.

There is a beautiful passage in the book of Job which is worthy of your attention at this point. The poor patriarch was afflicted with sudden bereavement, with poverty, with the fretful suggestions of his unamiable wife, and with the unjust reflections of his well-meaning but mistaken friends. Thus harassed, the good man looked to the Almighty, and taking a comprehensive view of his holy character, asked, "Will he plead against me with his great power?"

Then calling to mind the goodness of the God he loved, he answered his own question thus: "No; but he would put strength into me!"

Sublime faith! *Put strength into me!* Delightful assurance! Yet that is what God actually does to all who love him. Listen! Hear what he says to believers. These are his words: "Fear thou not: for I am with thee. I will strengthen thee; yea, I will help thee; yea, I will uphold thee with the right hand of my righteousness. I the Lord thy God will hold thy right hand, saying unto thee, Fear not; I will help thee!"

That this help is all-powerful you may learn by consulting the experience of good men in every age. The celebrated Colonel Gardiner is a notable example.

He spent his youth in a career of splendid but criminal follies. At thirty-one he was a prince among profligates, a chief among the worst of sinners, as godless as a demon. A tract awakened him. A dream terrified him. He repented, believed, was saved. Having been so long devoted to evil habits, it was natural for him to fear that temptations to his former pleasures would be too strong for his renewed nature to resist. But instead of this, so mightily did God help him, that "those licentious pleasures which had before been his heaven became now absolutely his aversion!" Speaking of this remarkable fact, his biographer says:

"I cannot but be astonished that he should be so wonderfully sanctified in body as well as in soul, as that from that hour he should find a constant disinclination to, and abhorrence of those criminal sensualities to which he fancied he was before so invariably impelled by his very constitution, that he was used strangely to think and to say that Omnipotence itself could not reform him without destroying that body and giving him another!" But it did help him to reform that ill-used body, and thus made him a notable example of the truth, that God not only promises to help, but that he actually puts strength into those who serve him, so that they are able to "overcome when they are tempted," and to come off "more than conquerors through Him who loved them and gave himself for them."

Perceive you not, therefore, beloved youth, the advantage which piety will give you in your struggles with those tendencies of your nature which endanger your moral safety in this life? What means of self-protection have you, as an unrenewed soul, that can be compared with the quickened conscience, the genuine self-respect, the holy love, the divine aid, which give so much moral power to the pious man? You have nothing, absolutely nothing. Come, then, my fellow immortal, be persuaded by your hopes of escaping the degradations which so often follow a life of sin this side the grave, to give yourself to Christ. By the fate of millions of ruined immortals, by your fears of social shame, and your dread of heart agony, I beseech you give your heart to Christ. Cry to God, saying, "Hold thou me up and I shall be safe." God will hear your cry, and then you will exclaim with David, "Thou art my hiding-place and my shield: I hope in thy word."

CHAPTER V.

THE DARK DAYS OF LIFE.

"Every roof," says Emerson, "is agreeable to the eye until it is lifted, and then we find tragedy, and moaning women, and hard-eyed husbands, and deluges of Lethe."

In somewhat similar vein Longfellow sings these sweetly sad lines:

> "There is no flock, however watch'd and tended,
>   But one dead lamb is there;
> There is no fireside, howsoe'er defended,
>   But has one vacant chair."

"Every man," says Bishop Hall, "hath his turn of sorrow, whereby — some more, some less — all men are in their times miserable. I never yet could meet with the man that complained not of somewhat."

"Man," saith the words of Holy Writ, "is born unto trouble as the sparks fly upward."

Thus, you see, philosopher, poet, theologian, and

the inspired word, agree in teaching that every human being must drink the bitter waters of grief, must tread upon the burning sands of the parched desert of affliction, during his journey through life. There is no escape for any man, for sorrow is the heir-loom of the human race. Physical disease, domestic infelicity, pecuniary trial, overwhelming misfortunes, painful disappointments, ill-requited friendship, mental disquietude, anxious cares, and cruel bereavements, stand, like fierce warriors, at the door of every man's habitation, ready to do the bidding of that high Providence which superintends human affairs, and metes out chastisements and retributions to all. These warriors do not all cross every man's threshold; neither do the same ones enter every house. But this much is certain, some one or more of them is sure to cross the precincts of every household, and to pierce the side of every creature of mortal birth.

You, then, beloved youth, must sooner or later feel the smart of the weapons of these providential warriors. Healthful, buoyant, and hopeful as you now are, it is difficult to impress you with this truth. Nevertheless, unless you are to be a sole exception in the history of your race—and of this you cannot even dream—you will, ere many years have passed, be the victim of heart-oppressing griefs.

Permit me then to ask you on what prop you intend to lean when the afflictions of your coming years shall weigh like a mighty burden on your trembling heart? By rejecting piety you cut yourself off from *Divine* support in your days of grief. Tell me, therefore, nay, tell your own self-injured spirit, to what it is to look in the years of coming sorrow.

Suppose, for instance, it should be your lot to suffer what is a very common fate in this land of commercial enterprise and speculation, the sudden wreck of your business affairs after enjoying years of success. Imagine your business bark well launched, wisely freighted, and prudently managed. She makes many a voyage, returning from each successive adventure more richly laden than ever before, until you begin to grow rich. Your prosperity continues long. You reach the full maturity of your manhood. You think of relaxing a little from the pressure of business occupations, for you are satisfied with your success, and have the means of living in calm repose the remainder of your days. But just as you attain the height of your ambition, the commercial sky is suddenly overcast; the whirlwind of monetary revulsion sweeps fiercely over the seas of business, tearing the sails of your richly laden bark to tatters, and driving her a dismasted wreck upon the rock of insolvency. You behold the battered fragments and exclaim, "I am a ruined man!"

In that hour, when the convulsions of a day shall swallow up the toils of a long life, and leave you, on account of exhausted powers, without hope of recovering your wealth and social position, what will you do without a God? What power will sustain your sinking heart? Whence will come the fortitude, the courage, the energy, which can bear you bravely on to the victory of mental repose through such a trial?

Perhaps you think your own *strength of mind* will be sufficient to sustain you in such adversity. Vain idea! Know you not that in such great emergencies the most self-reliant minds become weak, timid, paralyzed, and confounded. A fearful sense of impotence steals over them. Their reason reels, and shrinking from the terrible conflict with Providence, they either sink into imbecile melancholy, or plunge madly and unbidden into the mysterious presence-chamber of Deity. Let me give you a sad example of the latter result.

There were two merchant princes, brothers and partners, one of whom resided in New Orleans and the other in Mobile. Their wealth was immense, their experience large, their skill uncommon. A great monetary hurricane swept over the seas of commerce, and many a mercantile house perished, but their proud bark defied the storm and rode through it unharmed.

Time passed, and at a period when the business world was generally prospering, these merchant princes suddenly found their affairs embarrassed, and they failed. Overwhelmed by this great trial, one of the brothers plunged, like a madman, into the waters, and entered the presence of his Maker a shivering suicide. The other, on learning what his brother had done, followed his guilty example, and also rushed unbidden into the Eternal Presence! Thus these men, so strong, so self-reliant, and so long prosperous, found their great strength dissolved to weakness in the hour which tried their souls.

A scarcely less melancholy, but more striking

illustration of the insufficiency of mere mental strength to sustain a mortal man in the hour of unexpected calamity, is found in the life of Napoleon. On the day preceding the battle of Borodino, Napoleon was in excellent health and most joyous spirits. Late in the evening he received a dispatch informing him that his troops in Spain had been badly beaten at Salamanca. Immediately a singular change passed over him. In that disaster he saw the index finger of fate pointing to his final overthrow, and he was troubled. He retired to his couch but could not sleep. He arose, talked incoherently, ordered three days' rations to be distributed among his guard at midnight, and seemed to be consuming with fever of mind and body. The next day he was irresolute, ill-humored, and inferior to himself on the field of battle. In fact, the news from Salamanca overwhelmed him, and with all his strength of mind he staggered beneath it like a drunken man. It drove him to the brink of insanity. He showed very similar confusion of mind in the hours which preceded his abdication; and when his power was finally taken from him, his great heart grew sick, and on that sea-girt rock where British caution confined him, he pined away, and died as much of a broken heart as of the diseases which preyed upon his well-knit frame.

If, therefore, the strength of this gigantic soul, and of those lofty-minded merchants, was insufficient for their support in the great emergencies of their lives, what can *you* expect but to be crushed beneath *your* sorrows if you dare to confront them without the aid of God?

Perhaps you think that the sympathy of friends will give courage to your heart and energy to your will in your hours of calamity. But are you sure that adversity will not prove an enchanter's wand, and transform your friends into strangers? Is it not possible that, as the prodigal was abandoned, in his hour of misfortune, by those who smiled on him in his days of plenty, so may you be forsaken by those who now profess undying attachment to you? The falsehood of friendships is proverbial, and when the shadows of great trials darken your path, it may be your lot to meet

"That weary, wond'ring, disavowing look"

which prosperous selfishness knows but too well how to give those whose fallen fortunes render their friendship no longer desirable. In that case the staff on which you lean will become a serpent to wound your hand, and send its poison with throbs of agony into your bursting heart. Then you will comprehend the meaning of the poet, who, speaking of friendship, says:

> "Wake up the countless dead; ask every ghost
> *Whose* influence tortured or consoled the most;
> How each pale specter of the host would turn
> From the fresh laurel and the glorious urn,
> To point where rots beneath a nameless stone
> Some heart in which had ebb'd and flow'd its own?"

Ay, it is even so. From our dearest friends come our sweetest pleasures and our bitterest woes; for what grief can be compared with that which is caused by the discovery of heartlessness in those whom we have loved and trusted? There is no sorrow like it, as David confessed when his harp wailed in melancholy unison with that bitter cry, "Had it been an enemy I could have borne it!"

I know you persuade yourself that *your* friends are true and will not so forsake you in your troubles. Perhaps they are, and yet it may be they are not. But admit them to be to you as Damon to his Pythias, or as Jonathan to David, how know you that they will live until the dark days of your adversity begin? or, if they live, how assure yourself that they too will not be as deeply immersed in the sea of trouble as yourself? Are they not the children of mortality? Is not their prosperity as uncertain as your own? How then can you wisely lean on human friendship to sustain you in the day of your great need? Would you advise a lame man to lean on a reed? Would you venture to cross a storm-swept lake in a boat of gossamer? Why then do you do what is equally foolish, rely on human friends whose lives are but as a vapor, who wither like grass and fade like flowers? Remember, my friend, the Creator of all men has said: "*Cursed be the man who trusteth in man, and maketh flesh his arm, and whose heart departeth from the Lord.*"

If it should be your lot to be *bereaved*, as many are, of friends, lovers, and relatives, to whom will you look for consolation? Death sometimes enters a man's social circle as the woodman does his field, cutting down every ancient tree and tender sapling, and leaving him, like a solitary tree, to cast his companionless shadow across the silent scene. Here is an illustration:

The master of a ship died, leaving a widow almost penniless, a sickly daughter, and a heroic son.

Deprived of her heart's truest love, the widow turned with affection and hope to her son. His filial eyes flashed responsive love, and his heart nerved itself to the task of comforting and supporting his mother and sister. He trod the deck of his dead father's ship, and gave large promise of early ability to fill his place as captain. But sickness smote his noble form while at sea. He returned a pale-faced invalid. Two days after his arrival at home his mother bent over his bed in speechless grief, his fragile sister sat weeping at the window. Suddenly the young man opened his languid eyes, and slowly said: "The—ship—is—sinking!" His eyes then closed forever. He was dead!

And with his death the widow's hopes were all wrecked. Her last earthly helper was dead. She was bereft of all save the helpless girl, whose sobbing grief only dropped wormwood into the gall which was in the cup she was forced to drink.

Place yourself, my dear reader, without Divine comfort, in that widow's place, and tell me how you would bear up such a load of woe. Do not evade by saying you may never be so bereaved, because you know it is almost certain, if you live to mature life, that you will be called to stand beside the death-beds of many, if not all, whom you now love best. Your patriarchal father, your precious mother, or those sharers with yourself of that sweet love-nest, a mother's bosom, your brothers and sisters, or that dearer self, your beloved companion, or that beautiful image of yourself, your own dear babe, or all of them may pass through the gateway of death before your eyes. What will you do in those terrible hours of grief? With no heaven-born faith to whisper God's loving promises in your ear, to pour the cordials of hope into your wounded heart, to infuse more than mortal strength into your staggering spirit, what will you do? Who will comfort you, when in your sorrow you ask,

"And shall I never more see loving eyes
Look into mine until my dying day?"

With the lights of your earthly life put out, and no beamings from heaven to illuminate your dwelling, what, O what will you do? The words of men will fall upon your ears like the creak of the rusty hinge on your chamber door, and you will be comfortless. Like the captive bird, dashing itself against the wires of its cage, until its poor little head and wings are sore and bleeding, you will bruise your heart against your great affliction. Perhaps you will exclaim, as did an impatient lady in her bereavement, "God gave me all, and took all from me. Fate, drop the curtain; I can lose no more."

Or with EURIPIDES you will sigh: "My heart is full of sorrow; there is no room for more."

Or, rising in malignant rebellion, you will wickedly cry, with a bereaved deist: "I intend to do all I can to revenge myself on the Almighty for the wrongs he hath inflicted upon me!"

At best, as an irreligious man, you can but chafe your bruised heart until it bleeds from every pore, and at length tutor yourself into dogged submission, feeling with one poet that

> "When we have learn'd the very worst,
> The spirit soon must yield or burst;"

and saying, perchance, with another:

> "Mute
> The camel labors with the heaviest load,
> And the wolf dies in silence.
> If they,
> Things of ignoble or of savage mood,
> Endure and shrink not, we of nobler clay
> May temper it to bear—it is but for a day."

But such submission will bring little comfort. It will deaden the poignancy of your grief by hardening your sensibilities, but it will leave your heart an arid plain, without a stream to refresh it or a flower to adorn it. O saddening prospect! O gloomy afternoon of a life that had so bright and hopeful a beginning! Pause, fond youth, and provide thyself with a covert from these foreboded storms, with oil for the healing of these inevitable heart-wounds, with a holy Comforter for these hours of mortal agony:

"Now in thy youth beseech of him
  Who giveth, upbraiding not,
That his light in thy heart become not dim,
  Nor his love be unforgot.
And thy God, in the darkest days, shall be
Greenness, and beauty, and strength to thee."

There are many other forms in which affliction may visit you, for it is a dragon with many heads. You may, to suppose one more case, be made the victim of some torturing disease, which may seize you with a grasp as harsh as that of an executioner of the Inquisition, and so severe as to thrill you with exquisite pain, and so enduring that your slow wasting life may become one long agony. In such a case of what value would wealth, friendship, human sympathy, mental strength, or aught else of earthly origin, be to your poor imprisoned spirit? Alas, nothing! Unsupported by Divine comfort, your inner life would be more painful than your outward sufferings. Lashed into a perpetual tempest, your feelings would dash against your trials, like angry waves surging upon the rock-ribbed sides of an ocean isle; and your soul, like a foundered ship, would sink into a great deep of fathomless despair.

Having thus faithfully, though faintly, set before you your prospects, as an impenitent sinner, under the probable afflictions of coming life, let me now lead you to the contemplation of a brighter picture, by showing you what piety would do for you in such afflictions as I have described.

At the battle of Wagram Napoleon rode slowly along the front of his troops, mounted on a snow-white charger. Shots were flying about him in every direction, and many who beheld him expected every moment to see him fall from his horse. But he rode as undisturbed amid the horrors of that terrible battle-field as he would have been at a mere parade. Why was this? *Napoleon believed in fate.* In his opinion the ball that was to kill him was not cast; or if it was, it was useless to attempt to escape its range. This belief kept him calm in the midst of the most appalling dangers.

In the battle-field of life, with changes, risks, dangers, and troubles on every side, the pious man maintains a similar but far nobler serenity of mind. *His mind is possessed by a sense of security.* He feels confident that no real harm can befall him. He may have malignant enemies, business may be uncertain, domestic trials like sharp arrows may pierce his breast, disease may be tugging on the strings of his life, the waters of affliction may be breaking in proud waves against his dwelling, yet he feels safe. Why? Does he, like Napoleon, believe in fate? Nay. But he does believe that God is pledged to protect him. "The eternal God is his refuge, and underneath are the everlasting arms," and that God whom he trusts has said to his heart, "Fear not; for I have redeemed thee. I have called thee by thy name, thou art mine. When thou passest through the waters, I will be with thee; and through the rivers, they shall not overflow thee: when thou walkest through the fire, thou shalt not be burned; neither shall the flame kindle upon thee." Isa. xliii, 1, 2. Hearing these words of assurance, he goes through the thick of life's battle, singing:

"Go, then, earthly fame and treasure;
Come disaster, scorn, and pain;
In Thy service pain is pleasure,
With thy favor loss is gain.
I have called thee, Abba, Father,
I have set my heart on thee;
Storms may howl, and clouds may gather,
All MUST work for good to me."

A dew-drop, falling into the sea, beheld the wild waves with terror, and cried, "I perish in this grave." But an open shell received it, and that drop of dew

"Into a pearl of marvelous beauty grew."

Shortly after a diver tore the shell from its ocean-bed, and then the pearl cried, "Now I perish quite!" But scarcely had it finished its complaint, before it found itself shining the "chief jewel in a monarch's diadem."

In this beautiful fable you see one interpretation which piety would enable you to put upon your afflictions. They might alarm you at first, but when at length you fully comprehended that as the dew-drop grew into a pearl through its dreaded immersion, so your troubles would grow into a "far more exceeding and eternal weight of glory," you would extract joy from grief, and pleasure from pain.

Would it not sweeten every bitter drop in the cup of your affliction to see in it the element of one of the pearls of your future crown?

Another use of affliction which you would discover is suggested by the following illustration.

An adventurous hunter, having visited the interior of Africa in search of game, often noticed a little gray bird twittering and chattering on the branch of the nearest tree. It seemed greatly excited, and anxious to attract his attention. When it had fairly won his notice, it darted forward in wavy lines, still keeping up its incessant twitter, as if inviting him to follow its flight. Allured by its strange manner, he one day followed it until it reached a hollow tree. Hovering over this tree a moment, it pointed to it with its bill, and then, quietly perching on a neighboring branch, watched his movements. Guided by the action of the bird the hunter looked into the hollow of the tree, and found a nest of wild bees well stocked with honey and wax. He afterward learned that this little chatterer was named the "honey-bird," and that the natives were in the habit of relying upon its guidance when in quest of the sweet stores of the bees.

Now, just what that honey-bird was to the hunter, affliction will be to you if you become a Christian. It will attract you from selfish pursuits to sweet stores of religious joy; it will lead you out of yourself and into God. In your earlier experiences you may be perplexed at times to know its purpose, but you will soon learn to recognize it as your heavenly Father's messenger-bird to conduct you to richer storehouses of his grace, and you will learn with Paul to say: "*He chastened us for our profit, that we might be partakers of his holiness.*" Is not this perception of the purpose of affliction also calculated to promote your joy in grief?

An example or two of believers in affliction, taken from actual life, will convince you that these views are not mere theories. Look first at a Christian on the rack of long protracted pain.

Many years ago a poor cripple had his abode in a comfortless hovel near the entrance to a large church. His limbs were so paralyzed he could neither sit upright in bed, nor raise his hand to his mouth, nor turn from side to side. Could outward circumstances be more unfavorable to happiness? Yet this poor SERVULUS was one of the happiest men in the place.

Unable to read himself, he begged every pious man who visited him to read to him from his Bible, and thus made himself acquainted with most of its contents. Amid unceasing sufferings, and through many years, he spent most of the time in praising God. And when his hour of departure arrived, he joined his watchers in singing a psalm. Suddenly he ceased and cried aloud:

"Hush! hear you not how the praises of God resound in heaven?" and forsaking his deformed earthly tabernacle, he became the occupant of a mansion in heaven. Did a wicked man ever endure such pain and poverty as this with such patience, contentment, and joyfulness? Never, since God made man!

Now go with me for a moment, in imagination, into yonder humble cottage. Hush! Tread softly! We are in the chamber of human suffering. See that pallid youth bolstered up in the arm-chair. The dew of death is on his pale brow. How he gasps for breath. O, it is hard work to endure the pain which racks his wasted body. The spectacle wrings bitter sobs from his agonized father, who stands beside him overwhelmed with grief. The old man's tears move the sick youth's sympathies, and gathering up his little remaining strength, he whispers, while a seraphic smile plays upon his thin lips:

"IT'S ALL RIGHT, FATHER. IT'S ALL RIGHT!"

It's all right! Yes, that youth's eye of faith looked into God's heart of love and saw its love-beats; saw that love permitted those afflictions, and that love would reward his patient endurance of them with an eternal weight of glory. With that perception it was easy to submit; easy to feel and to say, "It's all right, father!"

This perception is given to all the children of faith, and it works a *submission to affliction* in every form, which robs it of half its severity. It is the resistance of the will to trouble which gives it its chief power to wound, and that power is taken away the moment the mind consents to suffer quietly, on the ground that its highest interests are to be surely promoted by the suffering. From such submission flow consolation, strength, and elevated character. It is a silvery stream of bliss running through a heart in which flowers and shrubs have been blackened and burned by the flame of fiery trials.

How superior is this submission to that dogged necessitated submission which is the highest attainment of the impenitent mind! The latter is undignified, morose, cold, and unrefreshing. It is, in fact, only a negative submission, by which the man merely ceases to dash himself upon the bosses of God's buckler. But the former is a real submission, by which the believer consents to drink the cup put into his hands, because heavenly love wills it, and assures him that it is only bitter medicine necessary for his soul's healing. With this assurance he drinks it cheerfully, and then nestles in the bosom of the Omnipotent, singing:

> "Bless'd be Thy hand, whether it shed
> Mercies or blessings o'er my head;
> Extend the scepter or the rod,
> Bless'd hand! 'tis thee, thy hand, my God!"

Consider, therefore, beloved reader, whether the value of piety, as a light in the dark days of life, is not one of its most precious commendations. I have shown you that the coming of such days is as certain as the fact of your existence; that as a worldling you will have no real comforter amid their terrors; and that piety will bring you abundant sources of sweetest consolation. What then will you do? Will you continue in your sins, and sink in despair in the sure-coming hours of grief? God forbid! Will you give your heart to God, saying from this time, "My Father, thou art the guide of my youth?" God be praised! for by so doing you become invulnerable to the shafts of that sorrow which worketh death, and you will learn to sing at all times this song of faith and hope:

"I will not let Thee go, thou help in time of need!
Heap ill on ill,
I trust thee still,
E'en when it seems as thou wouldst slay indeed.
Do as thou wilt with me,
I still will cling to thee;
Hide thou thy face, yet, help in the time of need,
I will not let thee go!

"I will not let thee go; should I forsake my bliss?
No, Lord, thou'rt mine,
And I am thine;
Thee will I hold when all things else I miss.
Though dark and sad the night,
Joy cometh with thy light,
O thou, my Sun; should I forsake thy bliss?
I will not let thee go."

CHAPTER VI.

PLEASURES PECULIAR TO PIETY.

SOUTHEY, in his Chronicles of the Cid, relates a curious legend. At the dead of the night preceding a great battle between the Spaniards and the Moors, the inhabitants of Leon heard a mighty sound as if it were the tramp of a great army marching through their streets. This spirit army was nothing but the phantom of the excited imaginations of the people. Yet it broke their repose and disturbed their peace. And, in like manner, is the pleasure of a sinner broken by the march of his past sinful deeds through the chambers of his unpardoned spirit. Let him prosper like a Girard or an Astor, let him be gay as a Lothario, let him fill up the hours of life with the engagements of business or the excitements of pleasure, still there will be moments in which his senses will become dead to all external things, and his soul be compelled to listen to the unceasing march of his past misdeeds along the aisles of life. And then he trembles at the mighty sound, for his conscience whispers, "These are marching to meet thee at the judgment of Him against whom they were committed." Great is the unrest of such a soul, for it realizes that there is "no peace to the wicked," and without peace, of what value are all his gains and pleasures?

But *peace*, which is beyond the reach of the proudest impenitent sinner, is the inheritance of the weakest believer in Christ. It is given to him the moment he believes, as a legacy bequeathed him by the last will and testament of the Lord Jesus, in these delightful words: "Peace I leave with you, my peace I give unto you; not as the world giveth, give I unto you. Let not your heart be troubled, neither let it be afraid."

O how like the unruffled surface of a sunlit mountain lake is the breast of the man to whom this peace is given! God smiles on him and encircles him in his mighty arms, therefore his heart is at rest. No past sins march around the chambers of his spirit, for his offenses are all blotted out of the book of God; no voices of threatening murmur in his conscience, for he holds the "mystery of faith in a pure conscience;"

no fears of future retribution terrify him, for the Ancient of Days has said to him, "I, even I, am he that blotteth out thy transgressions for mine own sake, and will not remember thy sins." With the great apostle he stands at the cross and exclaims, "Therefore, being justified by faith, we have peace with God through our Lord Jesus Christ;" and with a sacred poet his glad heart sings:

> "A peaceful river softly flows
> In tranquil streams, to gladden those
>   Who put their trust in God.
> Within his holy place we feel
> The comfort of his presence still,
>   While oceans roll abroad."

What can the world offer thee, my young friend, that will compare with the preciousness of this divine peace? Is a lifetime of carnal delight worth an hour of such heavenly repose? Think! can gold, ambition, gluttony, lust, grandeur, or amusements compensate an immortal soul for its anxieties respecting the results of its conflict with God, and for the absence of the "peace of God?" It cannot be. Peace is necessary to true enjoyment. And peace is to be found only in the service of Piety. "Her ways," and hers only, "are ways of pleasantness, and all HER PATHS

ARE PEACE!" Enter her service and she will confer this precious peace upon you.

A delicate child once lost her mother at an early age. She was very affectionate, and the image of her sainted mother lived in her heart. Clinging to the neck of her lady attendant, she would frequently say, "Now tell me about my mamma!" After feasting on what she heard awhile, she would say: "Now take me into the parlor, I want to see my mamma!" Carried to the parlor, and placed on a sofa opposite a portrait of her mother, she would gaze for hours on the silent picture. But she was a frail flower, and the dew of death was on her brow. One day she became unconscious for hours. Then a sudden brightness broke over her pale face, her eyelids opened, her lips parted, her thin hands were stretched out as if reaching for some object which her eyes beheld in the distance. After a few moments she cried: "Mother! mother!" and expired.

In this touching fact you see the operations and power of *love*. Love was the life of that child. It was her soul's atmosphere. To commune with the memory of her mother was her meat and drink, her chief delight, her highest bliss. This was an earthly love, yet it illustrates the operations and power of that divine love which is brought into the heart of every believer in Jesus.

Love to Christ is the principal thing in piety. It is born in the moment of conversion, and when born it immediately becomes the life of the new-born believer and the mother of every Christian virtue. Like the child, he dwells with ever increasing delight on the character of his beloved, and communes, not with his *memory* merely, but with the Saviour himself, for "his fellowship is with the Father, and with his Son Jesus Christ." And that communion is real rapture. It stirs the depths of his emotional nature. It causes his heart-strings to give forth their most delicious music. It swells his soul with throbs of unspeakable joy. It makes him a participant of those pleasures which constitute the felicity of heaven. When not too happy to give expression in language to his joy, he sings with the poet:

"O love, thou bottomless abyss!
  My sins are swallowed up in thee;
Covered is my unrighteousness,
  Nor spot of guilt remains on me;
While Jesus' blood, through earth and skies,
Mercy, free, boundless mercy, cries.

"By faith I plunge me in this sea;
  Here is my hope, my joy, my rest;
Hither, when hell assails, I flee;
  I look into my Saviour's breast;
Away, sad doubt and anxious fear!
Mercy is all that's written there."

Let me give you a few testimonies, from the lips of the children of God, to the bliss of divine love. Hear AUGUSTINE. He says: "Come, O thou joy of my spirit! Let me behold thee, O life of my soul! Appear unto me, O my great delight, my sweet comfort! O my God, my life, and the whole glory of my soul! Let me hold thee, O love of my soul! Let me embrace thee, O heavenly bridegroom! Let me possess thee!"

See yonder cottage standing alone on the edge of a bleak, barren moor. The day is cold and stormy, yet a faithful pastor has just dismounted from his horse at that cottage door. He is going to visit the resident of the cottage. Let us enter with him. What a lone and cheerless room! The snow has been drifting through the roof, and under the door, on the uncarpeted floor. There is scarcely an ember burning on the hearth. Mark that old, trembling man, seated in a broken arm-chair, with an open Bible upon his knees. How serene his aspect! See the rapture in his eyes, the sweet smile upon his lips. Hark! The pastor speaks, and says:

"What are you about to-day, John?"

"Ah, sir," the happy old man replies, "I am sitting under His shadow with great delight!"

Sitting under His shadow with great delight! What an overflowing fountain of bliss must the love of Christ have been within that child of poverty to make him so sublimely superior to outward circumstances! No wonder that another holy man—the persecuted Rutherford—could say: "There is more to be had of Christ than I conceived. Christ is so good that I would have no other tutor, if I could have choice of ten thousand besides. The saints at their best are but strangers to the weight and worth of the incomparable sweetness of Christ. He is so new, so fresh in excellency every day to those that search more and more in him. O, we love an unknown lover when we love Christ!"

Such is the love which is the life of pious souls. It absorbs all their emotional nature, and satisfies its highest demands, for its object is the Infinite One. It is ever fresh, new, and increasingly delightful, because the manifestations of its beloved are constantly renewed, and are exhaustless as infinity. Its exercise calls forth the deepest and most exquisite feeling of which the human soul is capable. It kindles the flames of inextinguishable desire. There is nothing in merely human love worthy to be compared with it. Parental, filial, fraternal, conjugal loves, though refined and intensified by its influence, are but as stars of palest light to the midday sun when compared with it. It fills the soul and leaves it nothing to wish. It elevates, ennobles, and develops all that is great and beautiful in humanity. It raises the human to the divine, and by enabling the man to dwell in God, renders him so superior to changeful circumstances, that he can say with the strong-hearted Paul: "I am persuaded that neither death, nor life, nor angels, nor principalities, nor powers, nor things present, nor things to come, nor height, nor depth, nor any other creature, shall be able to separate us from the love of God which is in Christ Jesus our Lord."

Are you panting for enjoyment, my dear young reader? Would you drink deep draughts of the sweetest stream of delight that ever flowed through the human spirit? If so, give yourself to God, and let him "shed his love abroad in your heart." Then, and not till then, will you taste the true elixir of life.

Another pleasure of the pious heart may be seen in the following simple incident:

"See!" said a rich landowner to a poor peasant, as he pointed to the beautiful landscape around them; "those broad fields, those magnificent parks, those dense forests, those snug farms, and, in short, all you can see on every side, belong to me!"

The poor man looked thoughtfully a moment at the great landholder, and then, with the rapture of faith burning in his eyes, looking toward heaven he pointed upward and said:

"And is *that* also thine?"

The lord of that vast landscape was silent. Before the peasant's question the glory of his possessions faded into mist. His portion all lay this side the grave, which was the horizon of his grandest hopes. But the poor man, looking with the eye of faith upon his mansion in heaven, felt the rapture of a *hope* which brought the heavenly and the infinite into his bosom. His spiritual ear heard the Master saying, "In my Father's house are many mansions. I go to prepare a place for you." Believing these sweet words of holy promise, he rose into the consciousness of heirship to the divine, and his hopes reveled amid the richness, the beauty, the grandeur, the bliss of his imperishable inheritance. Thus hope shone upon the darkness of his temporary poverty, like the morning star upon the brow of night, and filled his soul with cheerfulness and strength.

Such a hope is the peculiar possession of the pious man. As an impenitent sinner you may taste the pleasures of earthly hope. Your imagination, hand in hand with hope, may revel amid beautiful pictures of your future greatness or happiness. It may lead you up the steep ascent of toil, and seat you on the empurpled chair of richly rewarded industry; it may conduct you, amid the plaudits of the many-throated crowd, to the bench of the magistrate, the seat of the senator, or the pedestal of the victorious soldier; it may picture you in the old arm-chair of the patriarch with her who is now, or soon will be, the "winsome" sharer of your joys and sorrows, and with your children and children's children in happy groups around you; or it may exhibit you, like another Newton or Milton, receiving the intellectual homage of mankind in return for some magnificent achievement of genius which you, it flatteringly whispers, are yet to perform. All this, and more, earthly hope may do for you without religion, for rich wine always sparkles in the full cup which she offers to the lips of her favorites. But she cannot afford you one pleasant anticipation when you attempt to peer into the life beyond the grave. As the owl closes her eyes when the daylight shines, so earthly hope shuts her eyelids when the brightness of the immortal world breaks upon her.

Moreover, earthly hope is the veriest flatterer and "will-o'-the-wisp" in the world. Rarely does she perform half she promises. She is also fickle as the wind, forsaking without a sigh all whom she deceives. Alas for him who fails to win the objects with which she enchants him! Hope leaves him desolate, dies in him, because, the earthly being lost, all is lost,

"And hope without an object cannot live."

Would you like to study the desolation of an unrenewed heart when hope forsakes it? Read with attention the following terrible lines:

"The tree will wither long before its fall;
The hull drives on though mast and sail be torn;
The roof-tree sinks, but molders on the hall
In massive hoariness; the ruined wall
Stands when its wind-worn battlements are gone;
The bars survive the captive they enthrall;
The day drags through, though storms keep out the sun,
And thus the heart will break, yet brokenly live on."

What pictures of despair! A withered tree, a wrecked hull, a rotten roof-tree, a ruined wall, prison bars, a sunless day, a broken heart! Yet thus did the hapless poet, writing from experience, describe the impenitent heart from which earthly hope has taken flight. The agony of the dying gladiator is tame in presence of this spectacle of a soul without hope.

But let us return to that divine hope which dwelt in the poor peasant's breast. She is an angel of life to every pious soul. Her promises are not flatteries, but sure words from the mouth of God. She charms not to forsake, but is faithful as the Eternal Spirit by whom she is begotten. All human friends may forsake the godly man, all earthly comforts be cut off, the spirits of all earth-born woes may hold a grim festival of grief under his roof, and wring from his tortured heart a wish for the coming of death; yet even then this divine hope will not abandon him.

As the angel sought the discouraged prophet of fire under the juniper-tree with words of cheer and food of mighty strength, so hope will bring him brightness, and power, and pleasure in his distress. Aided by her, he will look up from the lowest deep of human sorrow and sing:

"A country far from mortal sight;
Yet, O, by faith I see
The land of rest, the saint's delight—
The heaven prepared for me!"

A sublime illustration of the power of hope is found in the unique language of "Jack," a deaf mute, as given by "Charlotte Elizabeth." Speaking by signs—of course—of the day of judgment, he said God would open the book in which he had written all Jack's "bads;" God would find the page full, he said, but would not be able to read it. He would see nothing; for when he first prayed Jesus Christ had taken the book, and opening the wound in his hand, he had let it bleed all down the page, so that God could see none of Jack's sins, only Jesus's blood. Finding nothing against him, God would close the book, and Jesus would say, "My Jack!" put his arm around him, and bid him stand with the angels.

Beautiful conception! How strong, yet how simple was that child's faith! How delightful and full of cheer was his hope, founded upon it, of perfect safety in that day which is to try the souls of men!

Would you then, my young friend, taste the pleasures of heavenly hope? Give your heart to Christ! Would you possess that hope which anchors the soul so safely that it outrides the most terrific storms of life? Give your heart to Christ! Would you always carry the sweet singing bird of paradise in your breast? Give your heart to Christ! Thus will you share the delight of good old Rutherford, who, after enduring great trials with great enjoyment, said:

"At the beginning of my sufferings I had mine own fears lest I should faint. And I laid this before the Lord, and as sure as he ever spake to me in his word, as sure his Spirit witnessed to my heart that he had accepted my sufferings, he said to me, Fear not; *the outgate shall not be simply matter of prayer but matter of praise!*"

There are few pleasures so intoxicating to the mind as the *pleasure of victory.* To stand in presence of enthusiastic multitudes, as NAPOLEON stood in Paris after his first Italian campaign, to listen to the plaudits of impassioned thousands, to feel oneself the object of universal admiration, is, perhaps, to taste the most delicious fruit man can pluck from tree of earthly growth. All victories over difficulties which tax our powers to overcome them, yield a measure of kindred fruit. But more delicious still is the fruit of *victory over self.* He who conquers himself achieves a prouder conquest than Napoleon won at Lodi, Arcola, or Rivoli, for he overcomes a foe to whom even Napoleon was a slave.

Self is the most stubborn, crafty, and powerful of foes, harder to be won than Alpine passes or Russian Sebastopols. Yet he falls under the blows of every child of piety. Grace makes its possessor omnipotent in the conflict, because his arm is nerved by the Almighty "Christ that strengtheneth him." Principalities, powers, fleshly lusts, violent passions, powerful temptations, all fall before his faith, "which overcometh the world." His life is a series of victories, and therefore a series of pure and lofty pleasures.

In all solicitations to evil the great inducement to sin is the pleasure which the inordinate indulgence of some appetite or passion is supposed to yield. But how momentary is that delight! How speedily it is succeeded by the pangs of remorse and conscious self-degradation! When old HOMER pictured the guests of CALYPSO, after feasting at her luxurious banquets, changed into beasts, he taught a truth familiar to the thoughts of every self-enslaved man. Who ever tasted the pleasure of sinful indulgence without feeling that he had dragged himself down from manhood's fitting elevation toward the level of the brute—without calling himself the most witless of fools? On the contrary, who ever came out of a conflict with the flesh victorious, without a heightened sense of self-respect, a refreshing consciousness of power, and a peaceful elevation of spirit, yielding a thousandfold more delight than could be gained from the most unbounded indulgence? Would you taste this pleasure of self-conquest, my reader? Become a Christian, for this also is a pleasure peculiar to godliness.

Numerous other pleasures equally peculiar to piety might be named, such as communing with God in prayer, in his word, and in his ordinances. Then there are the pleasures of charity, such as feeding the poor, clothing the naked, visiting the sick, comforting the sorrowful, and leading lost souls to Christ. Last, but not least, are the delights of public and social worship, which are so exquisite to a truly pious soul as to fully justify the preference of a great monarch, who once said: "I would rather be a doorkeeper in the house of God, than to dwell in the tents of wickedness." And every spiritual worshiper can, without exaggeration, join the poet in this sweet and simple song:

"One day in such a place
  Where thou, my God, art seen,
Is sweeter than ten thousand days
  Of pleasurable sin.

"My willing soul would stay
  In such a frame as this,
And sit and sing herself away
  To everlasting bliss."

These facts and arguments must convince you, beloved youth, that if you would enjoy the highest happiness of which you are capable, you must enter the pathway of piety. If peace that passeth understanding, love that begets joy unspeakable, hope that brightens with immortality, consciousness of self-conquest, the delights of charity and of divine worship, are the peculiar and precious gifts of piety, your interests, to say nothing of your duty, require you to listen to her voice. Give heed, therefore, to her call. Enter her pleasant paths. Submit to her guidance. Let her lead you to the blessed Jesus, who even now is saying to you: "*Come unto me, all ye that labor and are heavy laden, and I will give you rest. Take my yoke upon you, and learn of me*," "*and ye shall find rest unto your souls; for* MY YOKE IS EASY, AND MY BURDEN IS LIGHT."

"O Lord! how happy is the time
  When in thy love I rest,
When from my weariness I climb
  E'en to thy tender breast.
The night of sorrow endeth there,
  Thy rays outshine the sun,
And in thy pardon, and thy care,
  The heaven of heavens is won.

"Let the world call itself my foe,
  Or let the world allure,
I care not for the world—I go
  To this tried Friend and sure.
And when life's fiercest storms are sent
  Upon life's wildest sea,
My little bark is confident,
  Because it holds by Thee."

CHAPTER VII.

HOW TO WIN VICTORY IN DEATH.

Two noble ships were sailing on the sea in a night of storm and darkness. The storm-spirit had not burst suddenly from the cave of the winds, but had sent avant-couriers across the sky through the afternoon in the shape of frowning clouds. In one of those ships these harbingers of danger, though noticed, had been but lightly regarded. In the other their warning glances had been the signal to prepare the ship for a conflict with the gale. In the first vessel everything went on as usual. No precautions were taken. In the second everything that prudent forecast could suggest was done. Relieving tackles were hooked to the helm, a spare tiller was got out, the binnacle lights were carefully trimmed, extra lanterns were lighted, and the ship made as snug as possible.

As the evening waned into night the storm broke fiercely upon the sea, and the two ships, under double-reefed topsails, were running before the gale. A steady helm was necessary to their safety. For a while both vessels ran grandly before the mighty breeze. But presently a huge sea broke over them and put out their binnacle lights. In the unprepared ship no extra lights were ready, and the compass was left in total darkness. The helmsman was perplexed, and the ship broached to. In the confusion the sea broke over her again, tearing away her bulwarks, sweeping her decks, and leaving her a helpless wreck. In a few hours she foundered, and nearly all her hapless crew were engulfed in the pitiless waters.

In the other ship, the moment after the binnacle light was put out a lighted lantern, ready for such an emergency, supplied its place. Her helm was kept steady. She was saved. A few days later, with all hands aboard, with sails all set and streamers flying, she glided into port, majestic as a noble swan.

These ships, with the opposite results of their respective voyages, are images of the opposite destinies which await human voyagers on the sea of life. Like the incautious captain, men may slight the clouds of admonition which flit across their sky, and sink engulfed in waves of ruin; or, imitating the prudent commander, they may heed the friendly warning, and sail in triumph into the calm haven of immortal repose. Indeed, the end of every mortal's life *must* be a fearful wreck or a great success. There is no middle course. A terrible cry of despair or a gladsome shout of victory *must* escape from the lips of every man when death dismisses his spirit from the chamber of life. Which cry he will utter depends upon the preparation he makes for that critical hour.

Now, my dear reader, let me remind you of the trite but solemn fact that *you* must shortly do battle with this great foe to life. The grim archer has the unerring shaft in his quiver which is destined to pierce your heart; or it may be even now on the string of his mighty bow. Who dares say it is not? In either case your hour of doom draweth nigh, for, as saith SCHILLER:

> "With hasty step death presses on,
>   Nor grants to man a moment's stay;
> He falls ere half his race is run,
>   In manhood's prime is swept away;
> Prepared or unprepared to die,
>   He stands before his Judge on high."

This is an unpleasant theme to you, young heir of mortality, I know. You do not like to contemplate this, your inevitable inheritance. Still, since you must enter upon it, is it prudent to avert your eye and refuse to give it consideration? Better, far better, to study it, tremble before it, and by timely preparation prepare to receive it with joy and not with grief.

When RACHEL, the great tragic actress, was dying, she caused her jewels and trinkets to be brought and placed before her on the bed. Their presence revived the memory of her public triumphs, for among the precious gems were the costly gifts which high-born nobles and puissant princes had laid at her feet. She gazed at them long and earnestly. Her eyes flashed, her pale cheeks flushed, and in piercing tones she cried: "Why have I to part with all this so soon?" and died!

Poor Rachel! all the treasures of her heart were in this world, and could not be taken with her into the next, for "shrouds have no pockets." Beyond the dark river she had nothing, for she had laid up no treasure there. No wonder she hugged life with the embrace of despair. She had everything to bind her to earth, nothing to attract her to the world beyond.

Here is another sketch. A rude old fisherman, speaking of death to a friend, said: "I know well enough that some rough winter night the old sea will be my grave—'tis not that I stand in dread of—'tis what a spirit may meet with if it gets a launch off from this shore with no notion how to make for the other."

These pencilings bring into relief two facts, which make death a disagreeable contemplation to all the ungodly. 1. In heaven they have no loved objects. 2. They have no spirit-kindled eye of faith to pierce the mists and vapor which float between the tomb and eternity. How different with the pious soul! His treasure is in heaven, for Jesus is the object of his affections, and his eye of faith beholds the cross of Christ spanning the mystic gulf which lies between every death-bed and the celestial city. To him, therefore, death is not a repugnant topic. He does not shrink from its contemplation. Nay, he loves to think of it, to desire it, to pant for it. As saith the poet:

"Rivers to the ocean run,
  Nor stay in all their course;
Fire ascending seeks the sun;
  Both speed them to their source:

So a soul that's born of God
  Pants to view his glorious face;
Upward tends to his abode,
  To rest in his embrace."

Is not this mental tranquillity in prospect of death a priceless blessing? Next to dying well is it not the most desirable of possessions? Were it yours would it not save you from many anxious thoughts, many painful apprehensions? Become a Christian and you will possess it, for one great purpose of the Saviour's death was "*to deliver them who through fear of death were all their lifetime subject to bondage.*"

But if your anticipations of death are painful, how terrible it will be to actually meet death! I do not affirm that you will be filled with terror in your dying moments; for like, perhaps, the majority of mankind, you may be unconscious in your last moments. As you know, many diseases cause delirium, somnolency, or paralysis. In multitudes of cases medical men administer opiates, which keep the dying in slumberous, dreamy, hallucinated conditions. Frequently men die suddenly or violently. A fit, a bursting blood-vessel, a rupture of the heart, a fall, a blow, an epidemic, a railroad or steamboat casualty, or some similar catastrophe, smites men down so swiftly that the hand by which they fall is to them invisible. In all such cases there is no consciousness, consequently neither joy nor grief, hope nor fear, delight nor terror.

Suppose it should be your lot to die in one of these unconscious states. Without a Saviour what will you do when death, having unrobed your spirit, you awake to consciousness in ETERNITY? Will it not be terrible to behold the frown of an angry God, to hear the voice of the avenger cry: "*He that is unjust let him be unjust still, and he which is filthy let him be filthy still;*" to be bound in chains of darkness, and cast into the lake of everlasting fire? But with a Saviour an unconscious death will be an awakening to the ecstasies of unending felicity. Prepare, then, O youth, prepare to meet thy God!

You may, however, be conscious when death comes to unseal the door of life's mysterious chamber, and to bid your immortal soul depart to meet its destiny. Yet even in that case, though you remain impenitent, I dare not affirm positively that the pangs of guilt will thrill your conscience, and the fear of approaching retribution terrify you. I wish to deal sincerely and frankly with you, and therefore I concede that many wicked men have no "bands in their death:" they die boldly, fearlessly, as the brute dieth. GIBBON, who cherished a bitter hatred of Christianity to the last, died tranquilly, and exhibited an almost perfect indifference as to his future welfare. HUME, the skeptic, conscious of his approaching death, spent his last hours in jocular conversation with his friends, and in reading amusing books. He met death without any apparent perturbation of mind. LORD NELSON, though reeking with the sin of unrepented adultery, died thanking God he had done his duty. MARSHAL NEY, who certainly was no Christian, marched into the presence of his executioners with the same serenity of soul and pomp of manner with which he had been wont to appear upon a parade ground. The GIRONDISTS, notable for their deism, feasted like epicures, and discoursed like philosophers, the night preceding their death. They went to the scaffold, and died singing the Marseillaise with astonishing enthusiasm. NAPOLEON, unrepentant of his splendid crimes, met death without the least uneasiness as to his future life. And these individuals are the representatives of large classes, who, in all spheres of life, and under every variety of circumstances, meet death in the full possession of consciousness, unsupported by religious faith, and yet without feeling those terrors which often rend the consciences of wicked men.

Do not think, however, that in their death such men resemble believers in Christ. There is a distance, almost infinite, between their stoical indifference, and the hallowed peace which reigns in the bosom of a dying believer. The highest triumph of the former is a mere negation; they merely succeed in excluding fear: while the latter not only conquer fear, but they attain to a positive joy, arising from the contemplation of that future which the former are obliged to forget in order to keep fear quiet. The former are not terrified, because they resolutely cover their eyes that they may not behold their adversary; the latter gaze upon the foe with open face, comprehend his utmost power, and yet triumph! The superiority of the latter over the former is, therefore, scarcely less than infinite. No man in his senses can deem such calmness as sinners feel in such an hour at all desirable. Yet this is the utmost victory that the proudest sinners can achieve in the hour of death. Such as it is they have it, either because they are ignorant of their true destiny, or because, if acquainted with revealed truth, they have put it from them until the "god of this world hath blinded their minds," and the God of heaven, by leaving them alone, "hath blinded their eyes, and hardened their heart," so that while "hell from beneath is moved" to meet them at their coming, they see no danger. Yet, as with the former class, "sudden destruction" awaiteth them. Behold the true character of their boldness in an illustration.

The peasant long familiar with the rumbling voices and fiery belchings of a volcanic mountain, builds his cottage on some green spot which the burning stream of past eruptions has left unscathed, and sleeps at night heedless of the mysterious warnings which the mountain mutters. The bellowing of the crater is as unnoted by that thoughtless sleeper as is the bubbling of the brook or the tinkling of the cow-bell by the dweller in the vale below. Years of security make his serenity appear like the fruit of the ripest wisdom, and seem to justify his scorn of those who warn him of the danger which surrounds his home. But at length the fiery waves rise up to punish his hardihood; and some fatal night, while he dreams of safety and smiles, red hot arms burst the breast of the mountain and drag him, with the smile upon his lips, to the burning lake beneath.

This is a faint image of a bold sinner's death. His courage is foolhardiness, his defiant glance at death is the expression of a reckless spirit. How quickly his bravery forsakes him when, forced from his defiled body, his guilty soul stands on the brink of everlasting burnings, when his offended Creator glances infinite indignation at him, and says: "Fear ye not me; will ye not tremble at my presence?" "Therefore, thus saith the Lord God, Behold I, even I, am against thee!" Then will he join the vain cry of guilty kings, great men, rich men, and mighty men, to the rocks and mountains, saying, "Fall on us and hide us from the face of Him that sitteth on the throne and from the wrath of the Lamb: for the great day of his wrath is come, and who shall be able to stand?"

But even this poor comfort of dying "as the fool dieth" is not permitted to all impenitent men. It may not be to you if you remain unsaved. The second death may cast a deep shadow on your trembling heart in that solemn hour, as it did on the spirit of one to whom I will now introduce you.

There lived a man whom God had endowed with the richest gifts of genius. His friends gave him all the advantages of the most liberal culture. He meddled with all knowledge. He wrote books and the world praised him. Learned men almost worshiped him. Princes contended for his presence in their dominions. Woman poured the wealth of her affections into his soul. Honor crowned his brow. Plenty emptied her cornucopia at his feet. Health breathed vigor into his veins, and made his life one long enjoyment. Time touched him gently, and he lived to see a green old age. Thus this man possessed everything but the smile of God. How did he die?

See him, gray-headed, gray-bearded, and venerable, seated in an easy chair near an open window. The weary wheels of life move slowly now. His limbs are feeble. His breathing is slow. Death is at the door of the chamber of life. It opens. The soul of the dying man is commanded to go forth—to enter the world beyond. A leaden seal closes his senses against terrestrial light, but no celestial light pierces his soul. He is startled, cries, "More light!" and dies.

Poor GOETHE! for that was his name, saw no brightness reflected from the world beyond to cheer his dying chamber. But instead, a horror of thick darkness settled upon him and wrung from his distressed heart that fearful cry, "More light!" "More light!" That cry was vain. It came too late. He had lived without God, and God left him to die in the dark. Poor Goethe! poor poet! His life was a brilliant day, ending in the blackness of an eternal night.

Nor is such a death as Goethe's, sad as it was, by any means as painful as that of many sinners. To some it is given to foretaste the agony of that damnation which awaits them. Blair had such before his eyes when he penned his thrilling description of a remorseful sinner's end. Listen to his painful numbers:

> "In that dread moment how the frantic soul
> Raves round the walls of her clay tenement,
> Runs to each avenue and shrieks for help,
> But shrieks in vain! How wishfully she looks
> On all she's leaving, now no longer hers!
> A little longer; yet a little longer,
> O might she stay to wash away her stains,
> And fit her for her passage! Mournful sight!
> Her very eyes weep blood, and every groan

> She heaves is big with horror. But the foe,
> Like a staunch murderer steady to his purpose,
> Pursues her close through every lane of life;
> Nor misses once the track, but presses on
> Till, forced at last to the tremendous verge,
> At once she sinks to everlasting ruin."

Do you think the picture is too deeply shaded? If so, read the following facts: A man who had long heard the Gospel preached was sick unto death. A minister of my acquaintance went to visit him. As he ascended the stairs his ears were startled by the dying man's cries of distress. On entering the room he saw two men beside his bed. One held his hands to keep him from gnawing them in his despair. The other kept his feet in bed. His face was the embodiment of horror. When he saw the minister he cried, or howled rather:

"O God, don't, don't! Thou just God, don't, don't, don't!"

After a time his howlings and violence ceased, and he lay with his face buried in the pillow, and moaning "Mercy! Mercy! Mercy!"

But no ear heeded his piteous cries; no voice came to quiet the terrible tumult in his agitated soul. He died with the guilt of a lifetime on his spirit. He was like those ancient Jews, who said, "We will walk after our own devices, and we will every one do the imagination of his evil heart;" and to whom God had said, "I will show them my back, and not my face, in the day of their calamity."

Listen again! Hear the death-bed cry of the great and worldly CARDINAL MAZARIN. "O my poor soul!" he exclaims, in piteous tones, "what will become of thee? Whither art thou going?" VOLTAIRE's death-chamber, as you know, was a scene of horror. PAINE's was both fearful and disgusting. RANDOLPH's dying experience was written in the thrice repeated word, "remorse! *remorse!* REMORSE!" a word which expresses more of mental agony than any other known to man. HOBBES, trembling with apprehension, said: "I am about to take a leap in the dark." DAVID W. BELL cried, "O I must be damned! I am damned! damned to all eternity!" A man named CHALONER died cursing, and crying, "O torture, torture, torture! O torture, torture!" Another, named ROGERS, exclaimed, "I have had a little pleasure, but now I must have hell for evermore. I must to hell, I must to hell! I must to the furnace of hell for millions and millions of ages!"

But enough of these sad pictures. They sicken my heart, and my pen trembles as I think that the fair youth who reads these pages may, by neglecting his soul, pass through such agonies to an eternal prison. "Forbid it, gracious Redeemer!" is the prayer which rises to my lips. Prevent it, precious youth, by knocking at the wicket gate which opens into the pleasant path of faith in the Son of God!

Do this, and then O how delightful it will be to die when the appointed hour strikes! A life of faith leads to the verge of heaven, as a good man's death-chamber has been truly called. To stimulate you to begin a Christian life now, let me sketch a few righteous souls engaged in victorious combat with the grim warrior of the "white horse."

When Mrs. Hamlin, a missionary in Turkey, was on her death-bed, her physical sufferings were intense. But amid all her agonies she said she had "perfect peace," and her one desire was "to reach her rest." Toward the last her pain of body ceased. An expression of ineffable peace settled on her features, and the tones of her voice, as she bade farewell to her husband, were tremulous with the tenderness of overflowing affection. At length she sunk quietly away as one falleth into a sweet slumber. Thinking she was dead, her husband exclaimed, "My Henrietta! my Henrietta!"

She opened her eyes, and looking earnestly around, asked, "What child is this? Is it little Carrie?"

"No, my dear," replied her husband, "there is no child here!"

"Yes," she rejoined, "it is little Carrie, and the room is full of children."

Then looking upward, she breathed her joyous spirit into the arms of the angels whose presence her half unvailed spirit had just before mistaken for beautiful children. Can the records of unrenewed mind furnish one example of such a beautiful death as this? I answer emphatically, NOT ONE! Such a death is impossible to an unregenerate mind.

Here is another case. It is cited by Dr. Moore. He stood by a dying believer, and asked, "Are you in pain?"

"It is delightful," was the reply.

Another of his patients was so overpowered with the love of God that he died saying, "This is life—this is heaven. God is life—I need no faith, I have the promise!"

MONTMORENCY, constable of France, died on the field of battle. "Die like a good Christian," said some of the members of his staff as they soothed his last moments.

"Gentlemen and fellow-soldiers," he replied, "I thank you for your concern about me, but the man who has endeavored to live well for fourscore years, can never have to seek now how to die well for a quarter of an hour. But my having endeavored to live well is not the ground of my dependence. No, my sole dependence is on Jesus Christ!"

With such noble words as these upon his lips the pious soldier ascended from the field of death to the mansions of eternal life.

Here is still another case. A gentleman named GOLDING was enjoying spiritual raptures as he was shaking off the garment of mortality. A friend who stood by with wonder in his looks, said:

"You seem to enjoy foretastes of heaven!"

"O," replied the dying saint, "this is no longer a foretaste, this *is* heaven! I not only feel the climate, but I breathe the fine ambrosial air of heaven, and shall soon enjoy the company!"

Shortly after his face wore an aspect of ineffable

joy, and crying, "Glory! Glory! Glory!" he ascended to nestle in the breast of Jesus forever.

And here is yet one more example. An aged man, after a long and very painful sickness, found himself dying. Taking his friendly watcher by the hand, he looked into his face with an expression beautiful as a seraph's smile, and said:

"I have just been down to the bank of Jordan to see how the water is. Methought as I stood there, old John Bunyan came, and tapping me on the shoulder, said, 'The water is deep or shallow in proportion as faith is in exercise.'"

Shortly after he whispered, "Come, Lord Jesus!" and closing his eyes slept sweetly in the Lord.

His faith was strong, and he found the waters shallow, as all do who have faith:

> "For, like a happy infant, Faith
> Can play among the graves."

These illustrations of the power of piety to give victory in death might be multiplied indefinitely. It is one of the peculiar results of the Christian life to teach its possessors to "die well." Not that every Christian dies equally triumphant, for there are degrees of triumph among dying believers, just as there are degrees of misery among dying sinners. But mark this, thou who must conquer or be conquered in death: the most timid Christian death is infinitely more desirable than the boldest death possible to a sinner; for the former is succeeded by immortal felicity, the latter by immortal misery.

Would you then escape the death of the wicked? Would you avoid the sudden plunge into damnation which awaits the sinner who dies in unconsciousness? Be pious! Would you be saved from the terror which thrills the spirit of the bold sinner, when death suddenly leads him to the lake of fire? Be pious! Would you be spared the dying agony of the conscience-stricken sinner? Be pious! Would you die peacefully, triumphantly? Be pious! Enter the way of peace; seek pardon; consecrate your young life to God; live a life of faith in the Son of God! Then, when the summons to die falls upon your ears, joy will swell your sanctified heart, and you will reply with the poet:

"Lo! I come exultingly:
What a triumph 't is to die!
All the bands of mortal life,
All the struggle, all the strife,

Death, and death's ignoble bed,
Underneath my feet I tread.

"Lo! I see, exultingly,
Visions bursting from the sky:
Glowing light from paradise
Gleams upon my ravish'd eyes;
Odors, sweeter than the spring,
Wafting zephyrs gently bring.

'Hark! the music steals along,
Welcome, sweet, of angel-song;
Now my spirit joyously
Mounts aloft, from bondage free,
Upward rising, high and higher,
Light as flame of heavenly fire.

"Through the open gates of light,
Streaming glory fills my sight;
I on blissful myriads gaze—
Stars of life! Seraphic blaze!
Swells my heart, my loosen'd tongue
Warbles an immortal song."

Dying thus you will realize that "godliness is profitable" even in death, which it transforms into a pleasant path and a peaceful way.

CHAPTER VIII.

LIFE BEYOND THE GRAVE.

After a week of storms I have not unfrequently looked on the noble bay into which the beautiful Hudson pours its abundant waters. Innumerable vessels of all sizes, from the graceful yacht to the stately ship, have met and charmed my eye. With their white sails all set to catch the favoring breeze, they have glided majestically as a flock of swans across the sunlit waves toward the great ocean beyond. "Those vessels," I have said, musingly, "are all alike outward bound. Each is steering for her destined port. But how opposite will be their fates. Some will outride every gale, escape every treacherous breaker, and proudly enter port; while others, dashed to pieces by the furious waves, or broken on pitiless rocks, will be most miserably wrecked."

And this is an image of the fates of men. When life is young, and fresh, and new, like the ships on the bay, they all glide on sunlit waters, sheltered by parental arms, and bound on a perilous voyage to that unknown sea, Eternity. But how diverse their destinies! Some, like prosperous voyagers, will reach the happy port and float on "seas of heavenly rest" forever. But many, alas! how many, will make shipwreck of life, and drift forever amid endless storms and darkness on seas of dark despair. One of these opposite destinies awaits them all, for there is no middle state for man in eternity. Perfect rest or absolute unrest, everlasting triumph or everlasting despair, heaven or hell, awaits every living soul at the end of the earthly life. *The wicked "shall go away into everlasting punishment: but the righteous into life eternal."*

God has made your soul immortal, a "picture of his own eternity." Indestructibility is stamped upon it. It is capable, therefore, of enjoying "everlasting life;" of suffering "everlasting punishment." But it cannot be destroyed. Its destiny is to be, to think, to feel, *forever!*

Forever! Did you ever look into that yawning depth making an attempt to sound it? FOREVER! Did you ever try to run a measuring line along the limitless ages contained in this mighty term? If so you know what it is to stagger on the brink of a bottomless abyss, to stand appalled in presence of boundless duration. Yet, since you must exist *forever*, permit me to enlarge your conceptions of this great idea by an illustration.

Suppose your Creator were to commission some tiny insect to remove the matter of this great globe to the most distant star in immensity. It can carry for a load only an atom so small as to be imperceptible to the eye. Millions of years are required for the performance of a single journey. It commences its task upon the leaf of a delicate plant. With its invisible load it departs, deposits it, and after millions of years returns for a second atom. What numberless ages would pass before that single leaf would be carried away! What untold periods before the whole plant would be gone! What vast cycles would elapse before a tree, a forest, a hill, a mountain would disappear! The strongest imagination staggers at the thought of the ages which would pass ere the last particle of the globe would be removed. Yet even then your imperishable spirit would be but in the infancy of its existence! Amazing thought!

"Immortal! Ages past, yet nothing gone!
Morn without eve, a race without a goal!
Unshorten'd by progression infinite!
Futurity forever future! life
Beginning still where computation ends."

This immortality is an attribute of your nature, and invests you with a grandeur which no earth-born greatness can equal; it stamps you with a value which defies computation; it imparts to your existence an aspect of terrible solemnity; it gives grave pertinency to the question of the great Teacher: "What shall it profit a man if he shall gain the whole world and lose his own soul?" and it justifies the inquiry of the poet:

"Round us, o'er us, is there aught
Which can fill our highest thought?
Aught which may deserve to be
With our noblest aims inwrought?
Yes, 'tis Immortality."

Since it is your destiny, immortal youth, to live forever, let me present you with a dim but faithful picture of life beyond the grave. Give me your hand! Let me lead you first to the brink of that perdition which will "move from beneath to meet you at your coming," if you continue in your present impenitent state until death. The spectacle may be painful to contemplate, but would it not be infinitely more so to be cast into that "lake of fire?" Look, then, that you may escape from it while escape is possible.

A prosperous sinner, who acquired large wealth, lived sumptuously, and dressed fashionably, was hurried from his magnificent dwelling into eternity. There was nothing notable in his death. He died as most sinners die, unconscious of the wickedness of his self-indulgent life and of the fearful doom which awaited him beyond the tomb. But scarcely had he closed his eyes on this world before he lifted them up "in hell, being in torments, and seeth Abraham afar off and Lazarus in his bosom. And he cried and said, 'Father Abraham, have mercy on me and send Lazarus, that he may dip the tip of his finger in water, and cool my tongue: for I am tormented in this flame.'"

"But Abraham said, 'Son, remember that thou in thy lifetime receivedst thy good things, and likewise Lazarus evil things; but now he is comforted and thou art tormented. And besides all this, between us and you there is a great gulf fixed: so that they which would pass from hence to you cannot, neither can they pass to us that would come from thence.' "

These, as you know, are the words of Christ. He knew what was in heaven and hell, because he was Lord over both. In giving this awful account of the rich sinner's fate, he pushed the gate of perdition open a little space that men might look in and see the misery of lost souls. That rich man is a representative character. What he suffers all lost souls suffer, all finally impenitent souls will suffer, *you* will suffer if you die in your present state. Fix your eye, therefore, on him in his "place of torment." Study his agony closely as a picture of your own future woe unless you repent.

"*I am tormented in this flame*," he cries. So fierce is his torment that to have the tip of his tongue touched by the wet finger of Lazarus seemed like a great favor. But even that trifling alleviation was refused as contrary to an unalterable law which formed an impassable "gulf" between his abode and the home of the redeemed.

What was the nature of the fire in which he was tormented? Was it material or mental? I cannot tell. God has elsewhere called it "*a lake of fire burning with brimstone*," and "*fire that is never quenched.*" Many good and wise men interpret these phrases literally. Others regard them as figurative, as teaching that the mental misery of lost souls is so intense that the exquisite pain which a man immersed in fire would suffer is the nearest representation that can be given of it. This is my own opinion. But how terrible must such anguish be! Look at that lost rich man again. See him writhing, weeping, tossing to and fro in the mysterious fire which burns without shedding one ray of light around his miserable abode! Hark how piteously he cries, "I am tormented in this flame!" Do you not shrink from tasting such woe? Do you not feel that it is "*a fearful thing to fall into the hands of the living God?*"

"*I am tormented in this flame.*" The fuel on which that flame feeds is the sin of his past life. His relations and obligations to God, with the ingratitude, the baseness, the folly, the selfishness, and the inexcusableness of his iniquities, are all fearfully transparent to his glaring eyes. His conscience, long sinned against, now "spits fire in his face and fills him with shame and horror." It peoples the murky atmosphere about him with ghostly images of his unrepented sins; it writes the half-forgotten record of his life in big fiery letters on the walls of his prison; it shouts the curses of the law in his ears; it reproaches him for his folly; it points him to the awful frown of his wronged, insulted, but now avenging Creator. Thus his conscience begets thoughts which float around him as a sea of unquenchable fire. Do you wonder that he cries, "I am tormented in this flame?"

When a guilty conscience is awakened *this side the grave* its pangs are like "the arrows of the Almighty," the "poison whereof drinketh up the spirit." What, then, must they be in a lost soul? Let me give you a few examples of these pangs, as felt by living men, arising not from a career of peculiar infamy, but from acts which are too often regarded as trifling and venial.

When SIR WALTER SCOTT was at school there was a boy in his class who always kept at the top. Scott long tried in vain to displace him. One day he noticed that, when questioned, this boy always kept his fingers fumbling about a particular button on his vest. Scott contrived to cut it off, and, as he expected, the next time the boy was questioned he missed both the button and his lesson. Scott got his place, but, as he afterward confessed, *the sight of that boy always smote him*, and he never ceased to wish that this un kind act had not been done.

A similar feeling of pain was once admitted by a sick youth, who, calling his father to his bed-side, said:

"Three years ago I told you a falsehood. *It has given me many sleepless hours.* I want to ask your forgiveness."

The pangs of an awakened conscience were very severe in the case of the REV. CHARLES SIMEON while he was under conviction of sin. His life had always been severely moral, yet, when "he saw the numberless iniquities of his former life, so greatly was his mind oppressed by them, that he frequently *looked upon the dogs with envy*, wishing, if it were possible, that he could be blessed with their mortality, and they be cursed with his immortality!"

A more striking case was that of an impenitent man who fell into a river and was so far drowned as to be insensible for some time. "What were your feelings when you fell into the water?" a friend inquired after he was restored to consciousness. He made this memorable reply:

"My feelings were the most horrible you can conceive. All the sins I ever committed rushed at once into my mind, and conscience portrayed the whole to me. I beheld the flames of hell kindled before me."

In some persons of extreme wickedness these pains of mind have grown so intense that the guilty sufferers have voluntarily confessed their crimes, after having denied them, on the scaffold and on the rack. "They have implored the mercy of a violent death as more tolerable than the agony of their guilty souls." Here is an illustration in point.

Two men were traveling in a retired part of the country, when one suddenly struck the other and slew him. Having robbed the body he concealed it and fled. Changing his name, the guilty man took up his abode in a quiet village, and having established himself in business, became a highly respected man and a magistrate. Many years rolled away, and he lived on unsuspected of crime. But one day, while trying a man charged with murder, his conscience, which for thirty years had been lashing him with cords of burning iron, asserted all its power. He could endure his concealed agony no longer. Stepping from the bench of the magistrate to the dock of the prisoner, he confessed his crime, and said:

"I cannot feel relief from the agonies of an awakened conscience, but by requiring that justice be done to me in the most public manner."

I have quoted these examples of the power of conscience to inflict the severest pain in this life, that you may see how such torment as the rich man suffered in hell may arise from the mind itself. A guilty conscience is itself a hell—a crater of flame kindled by the breath of an angry God—furnished with all the means of fiercest torment. A man's sins are the fuel which feeds the scorching flame. Imagination and memory are the remorseless tormentors ever toiling at the mouth of the sufferer's hell, and heaping his iniquities upon the undying fire. This is what Milton meant when he made his lost archangel say:

> "Me miserable! Which way shall I fly
> Infinite wrath and infinite despair?
> Which way I fly is hell; myself am hell;
> And in the lowest deep a lower deep,
> Still threatening to devour me, opens wide,
> To which the hell I suffer seems a heaven."

See you not, impenitent youth, in this feature of your moral nature, how you may be made a sad partner in that rich man's torment? If Sir Walter Scott was smitten with pain, through a series of years, by the recollection of a boyish act of injustice; if the sick youth was visited by sleepless hours during three years for a single falsehood; if the moral Mr. Simeon wished himself a dog when his iniquities met him; if, for more marked offenses, men have suffered beyond their powers of endurance in the flesh, what is there to save you from torment in the world beyond the grave, when your conscience shall be awakened by the hand-writing on the wall? When driven from the noise and occupations of this busy life; when the light of eternity shines unobstructedly on your naked spirit; when a resurrection of every buried act of sin shall take place in your memory; when a clear consciousness of the infinite love of God, which you have despised, shall awake within you; when a full comprehension of all you have been, and all you ought to have been, shall possess you; when the startling conviction that you are utterly, hopelessly, and eternally lost, arises within you; then, O then, will you not taste the rich man's anguish, and cry, "I am tormented in this flame?"

In addition to these gnawings of guilt, lost souls suffer from their intercourse with each other. The rich man dreaded the coming of his brothers to his place of torment, doubtless, because he shrunk from their reproaches. Hell is an association of wicked souls. Lost angels and ruined men are there linked in one vast society. What a thought! What profane blasphemies, what horrible curses, what mutual reproaches, what malignant speeches, must forever mingle with that "weeping, wailing, and gnashing of teeth" which characterizes them all! This fact alone makes my soul hasten far from the road to hell. To be the forced companion of all the blasphemers, infidels, thieves, murderers, liars, riotous and ungodly wretches who have cursed the world with their presence, is of itself sufficient to call forth an earnest purpose to avoid their abode. "O my soul, come not thou into their secret; unto their assembly mine honor be not thou united!"

Besides all this the rich man was the spectator of the bliss of heaven. He saw "Abraham afar off and Lazarus in his bosom." You are thus taught that lost souls are tormented by the sight of the heaven they have rejected. They can lift up their eyes from afar and behold the blissful land, the mansions, the innumerable multitude of the redeemed walking in white, the throne of God and the Lamb, only to be reminded that they too might have been inheritors of that bliss, but for their own obstinate rejection of the love which stooped even to the humiliation of death to save them. And ever as they look on the glorious brow of the adorable Redeemer, they shall hear a voice saying, "Ye would not come unto me that ye might have life." And when the echoes of the song of the saints floating across the impassable gulf shall fall upon their ears, saying, "Blessing, and honor, and glory, and power, be unto Him that sitteth upon the throne, and unto the Lamb, for ever and ever," they shall writhe with renewed torture. The "for ever and ever" in that song shall ring as the knell of eternal death, and thrill the wretched multitude anew, by reminding them that there is to be no end to their sufferings. "*The smoke of their torment ascendeth up for ever and ever; and they have no rest day nor night.*"

Once only in their weary life will the monotony of their woe be broken. On an appointed day the blast of an archangel's trump will summon them to the bar of the Ancient of Days, and to a reunion with their sin-defiled bodies. There, in presence of an assembled universe, they shall be "judged according to their works;" there they shall be condemned; there a reluctant confession of the justice of their doom shall be wrung from their lips; there, bowing the knee before the Lamb, whose atonement in their earthly lifetime they rejected, they shall publicly acknowledge the justice of God in their condemnation; and there, covered with "shame and everlasting contempt," they shall hear the once Crucified pronounce their sentence, saying, "Depart from me ye cursed into everlasting fire, prepared for the devil and his angels." They shall then be "cast into the lake of fire" to suffer the bitter pains of the "second death," without mitigation or hope of relief for ever and ever.

Such is the life of lost souls according to Holy Scripture. Such will be *your* life beyond the grave, dear impenitent youth, unless you become a believer in Christ. Can you bear the thought of thus "*drinking of the wine of the wrath of God?*" Do you not shudder at the bare idea of being thus "tormented" in the "presence of the holy angels, and in the presence of the Lamb?" Are the "pleasures of sin," which are but for a season, worth such a tremendous price? You would not leap into a den of hungry lions or hissing serpents, neither would you cast yourself into a fiery furnace; why, O why, then, will you walk the road which leads to the den of devils and lost souls? to the lake of fire which is as unquenchable as the life of your immortal spirit? O, pity yourself, and turn away, I beseech you, turn from the broad way, saying:

> "Nothing is worth a thought beneath,
> But how I may escape the death
> That never, never dies!
> How make mine own election sure;
> And when I fail on earth, secure
> A mansion in the skies."

LIFE, LIFE, ETERNAL LIFE! How cheering these words sound after the dreary voices from hell's everlasting prisoners to which we have been listening! Sadly has my mind traversed the scenes my pen has just pictured. Again and again my excited sympathies have bid me leave the picture unfinished, but the conviction that this view of the dark side of the life beyond the grave might move some precious youth to shun it, has restrained me. But having drawn it, I turn to the bright side of that life with the feelings of one passing from a charnel-house into the pure atmosphere of a bright summer morning. Give me your hand again, my reader. Let me lead you from the brink of perdition to the glorious land of Beulah. Let us stand beneath the trees of that pleasant realm, and while breathing its clear, balmy air, let us behold the children of piety as, emerging from the river of death, they ascend the shining path beyond it to the celestial city.

I have already shown you how believers die. Jesus has drawn aside the vail which hides the spiritual world from mortal observation sufficiently to let us see how, after escaping from their "earthly house," they ascend to heaven. Read! "And it came to pass that the beggar died, and *was carried by the angels* into Abraham's bosom!"

Carried by the angels! I thank thee, Jesus, for that revealing. It shows me how all believers reach their home, for surely Lazarus was not taken thither by any unusual method. *Carried by angels!* Delightful mode of transit! Borne, O how rejoicingly and lovingly! in the strong arms of "shining ones," the freed believer is in an ecstasy of unspeakable delight. Not a fear stirs the perfect calm which pervades his sprinkled conscience. Too happy to speak to his heavenly attendants, he looks steadfastly on the doors of his "Father's house." One thought fills his swelling soul: "I am saved! I am saved! I have fought the good fight, I have finished my course. Henceforth there is a crown laid up for me. O halleluiah! halleluiah to God and the Lamb for ever!"

Swimming in this delicious consciousness as in a sea of bliss, he finds himself in the celestial city, and is led through the long lines of shining ranks toward the presence of "our God which sitteth upon the throne" and "of the Lamb." As the beatific spectacle gradually unfolds its glory to his unaccustomed eye, he may say to himself,

> "And is this heaven? And am I here?
> How short the road! How swift the flight!
> I am all life, all eye, all ear;
> Jesus is here, my soul's delight."

He is before the throne. Ineffable love beams upon him from the glorious face of his Redeemer. There he is "clothed in white raiment," a palm is placed in his hands, Jesus "confesses" him "before his Father and before his angels," gives him a "crown of life," presents him with the "mansion" prepared for him, and joins him to the "great multitude which no man could number." Thus introduced to the life of heaven, he lifts up his voice and swells the everlasting song, saying, "Salvation to our God which sitteth upon the throne, and unto the Lamb!"

Who can conceive the unspeakable rapture of a saved soul during these first moments of his heavenly life! There is the consciousness of being actually saved, of dangers all escaped, of battles all fought, and victory won; of temptations, doubts, fears, crosses, trials, infirmities, cares, all left behind with the earthly house; there is the overwhelming gratitude, the adoring, subduing, clinging, burning love for his Saviour which swells in his soul, and bursts from it, like gushing springs, in songs of praise, as he feels through all the pulsations of his being the power of the thought, "I owe all this to Jesus!" This rapture is heightened by a profound sense of personal unworthiness which begets the wonder why he died for me. While, to crown the whole, comes in the idea of perpetuity. "This bliss is to endure forever!" his enraptured soul will say, and then, with immeasurable tides of blissful feeling sweeping through his nature, he will cast his crown at the Saviour's feet and sing:

"Unto him that loved us, and washed us from our sins in his own blood, and hath made us kings and priests unto God and his Father; to him be glory and dominion for ever and ever."

I love to think of a soul's first hour in heaven; for it seems to me that almost an eternity of bliss is included in its exquisite experiences. If all its subsequent life were to be spent with less of thrilling delight, that hour would atone for all the sufferings of its earthly past, and, as a recollection, be a star of beauty shedding joy forever upon its path. But, O delightful thought! the capacities of saved souls are destined to be endlessly developed, and to drink in ever-increasing draughts of bliss from the inexhaustible fullness of the blessed God. Its first hour in heaven is therefore only a prelude to a life of immortal delights.

The precise manner in which saved souls will spend their heavenly life is not revealed. What their duties will be, by what ministries of love their powers will be tasked, by what means their intellectual and moral progress will be promoted, the special relations they will sustain to one another, and how they will be distributed in the heavenly kingdom, are problems which it has not pleased God to solve for us who dwell in houses of clay. Nor will I speculate upon them, because enough of the heavenly life is revealed to make it an object of supreme desire.

In the heavenly life every cause of painful feeling will be absent. Read the beautiful statement of the Spirit respecting saved souls: "*God shall wipe away all tears from their eyes; and there shall be no more death, neither sorrow nor crying, neither shall there be any more pain.*" *No more pain, either of mind or body, to all eternity!* What a stupendous consolation!

On the other hand there is to be fullness of joy for evermore. God and the Lamb will anticipate and satisfy every want of their nature. Every intellectual aspiration will be gratified in the study of God's infinite being and productions, for they "shall SEE HIM AS HE IS." Every desire of the affections shall be met with delightful response, for to them shall be unfolded the meaning of that unfathomed truth, "GOD IS LOVE." Every shape of perfect beauty shall charm the eye, and every sound of richest melody shall delight the ear. Read the gorgeous imagery by which the Revelator vainly sought to convey his impressions of the perfect purity and perfect bliss which he beheld in his inspired visions. Having read it, then consider his authoritative assertion: "IT DOTH NOT YET APPEAR WHAT WE SHALL BE!" After all God has revealed of heaven, the heights of its joys have never been scaled, the depths of its delights have never been fathomed. Eye hath not seen it; ear hath not heard it; nor hath human mind conceived it. It must be enjoyed to be understood. Truly did the poet sing:

"We speak of the realms of the bless'd,
Of that country so bright and so fair;
And oft are its glories confess'd,
But what must it be *to be there?*

"We speak of its pathways of gold,
Of its walls deck'd with jewels so rare,
Of its wonders and pleasures untold—
But what must it be *to be there?*"

Such, immortal youth, is life beyond the grave. To the impenitent who do not obey the truth it is "*indignation, wrath, tribulation, and anguish.*" To those who believe in the Saviour it is *honor, glory, and eternal felicity.* Which of these vast extremes it will be to you depends on yourself. It is the will of Him "who loved you and gave himself for you," that you should inherit the latter. But he leaves you free to make your own choice. As you sow so shall you reap. Sow to the flesh, remain impenitent, seek your chief good in the earthly, and you *must* reap the torment which fell to the lot of the rich man. Sow to the Spirit by repentance, faith, love, and obedience, and you shall reap the unimaginable bliss of heaven. To sow to the flesh and expect to reap eternal life, is as foolish as it would be to expect to gather a crop of figs from the sowing of thistle-seed. If you sow the wind you must reap the whirlwind.

Which will you do? I advise, yea, I entreat you to sow to the Spirit, for I know you cannot endure to lie down in everlasting burnings. I know you must desire your own happiness in eternity. Flee, then, from the broad road in which you are now walking. It leads to DEATH. Rush from it as you would from the railway track if you saw the train dashing upon you. By all your dread of pain, by all your love of happiness, forsake it! By the value of your immortal soul, by the love which gave the "only begotten" for your salvation, by the love of Him who laid down his life for you, I adjure you, forsake the path which leadeth unto death, and enter the way which leadeth unto life. And what thou doest, do quickly, for "the time is short."

"There is a death whose pang
  Outlasts the fleeting breath;
O what eternal horrors hang
  Around the second death!

"Thou God of truth and grace!
  Teach me that death to shun;
Lest I be banished from thy face,
  For evermore undone."

CHAPTER IX.

I PRAY THEE HAVE ME EXCUSED.

In his beautiful parable of the great supper, the divine Teacher held a mirror before the hearts of impenitent men who are intellectually convinced of their duty, in which is reflected the grand reason why they do not turn to Him. The invited guests to that supper are described as sending in various excuses. One wished to feast his eyes on a newly-purchased piece of ground; another wanted to put a recently-bought yoke of oxen to the test; a third pleaded the privileges of a bridegroom. These excuses are so transparently frivolous that no reflecting reader can fail to see that *want of inclination* was the true reason why these persons declined to be guests at that supper. Had either of them possessed a spark of desire to be present, the alleged difficulties would either not have suggested themselves, or, being suggested, would have been pushed aside as mere pebbles from their pathway.

And is not *want of inclination* also the parent of your excuses for neglecting your salvation, and the grand reason why you stay away from Christ, my dear young reader? Your sober judgment is convinced that your happiness, your safety, and your duty all point to the path of piety. Look, then, into the secret workings of your heart; be true to yourself; drag your skulking motives from behind your array of excuses into broad daylight, and see if *an absolute disinclination to the service of Christ* is not the force that holds you back from him? Study yourself, and see if your inclinations are not all running in the channels of worldliness and self-gratification? Tell me now honestly, frankly, but for your disinclination to religious duty would not all the excuses which drop so trippingly from your tongue become lighter than the breath with which you utter them?

It may be, however, that the deceitfulness of sin so obscures this disinclination that it is not clearly visible as yet to your self-inspective eye. If this is so, then your excuses may be mixed with sincerity. They may bear with more or less weight upon your volitions, and it may benefit you to see them placed in the scales of truth. Will you permit me to weigh some of them therein?

Perhaps you shrink from *the prospective duties of a religious life.* You are unprepared for the sacrifices it involves, for its probable requirements at your hands, and therefore you say, "I pray thee have me excused." The following fact may embody the spirit of your excuse.

A young man of prepossessing aspect, intelligence, and respectability, once visited my house as an inquirer after Christ. He was the subject of powerful spiritual awakening, and was, so far as I could judge, entirely sincere. I did my best to lead him to Christ, but he found no peace for several weeks. I then concluded that some concealed difficulty stood between him and Jesus. Pressing him closely, I drew from him the confession that *a conviction of his duty to preach the Gospel after becoming a Christian* had sprung up in his heart. This was opposed to a darling plan of life which he had marked out for himself, and which he could not persuade himself to abandon. O how I pleaded with that noble youth to yield to his conviction and to present himself unreservedly to the Saviour! But I failed. The pride of his heart was too strong, too stubborn, to be subdued even by my great Master, and the young man ceased to be a visitor at my study. He remained a sinner; an amiable, moral, attractive young man, but impenitent and disobedient to God. Mark the result! Within two years a violent fever prostrated his manly form, beclouded his brilliant intellect, consumed the oil of his physical life, and sent his rebellious spirit unpardoned into the presence-chamber of Him to whose bidding he had replied, "I will not."

Let this young man stand on the plains of life, like Lot's wife in her shroud of salt on the vale of Sodom, a warning to all who, like him, excuse themselves from coming to Christ because of some unwelcome prospective duty. What if my reader, after being converted, will be called to speak of God's goodness, to visit the sick and the poor, to exhort, to preach the Gospel, to become a missionary, or to employ his skillful fingers and fertile brain in acquiring money for the use of Christ? Does the certainty of such a call dissolve his obligations to become a Christian? Besides, who and what are you, precious youth, that you should count any labor a disgrace, or a burden even, which Christ can require at your hands? Are you not his creature? Are you not so absolutely a pauper in his presence as to own nothing in the universe? Why, your very person belongs to him, and you are honored by any task, however lowly, which he may assign you. Place, then, the pride of your poor spoiled heart beneath his feet, and let him crush the foolish bubble. Tell him you count it greater honor to wash the feet of his meanest disciples than to continue in your sins. And remember that the seeming difficulties of religious duties will mostly vanish the moment you are converted. The Divine love shed abroad in your heart at that auspicious moment will make all things easy. It will inspire motive, impart strength, and make all duties not only possible but pleasant. Away, then, with such excuses if you have cherished them. But if you will persist in hugging them to your heart, fail not to see your destiny mirrored in the end of that youth to whom an excuse of this class was the millstone which dragged him from the foot of the cross down to regions of endless despair.

It may be that *fear of the ridicule of your associates, of persecution from your personal friends or family connections*, or of some other evil which terrifies your imagination, is your excuse. Admitting your sincerity, I beg to whisper a word or two in your ears by way of warning you against yielding to that cowardly emotion, fear.

Fear is of all things the most to be feared. It never stimulated any man to noble deeds, never achieved a triumph. On the contrary, it chills the heart, paralyzes the arm, petrifies every manly aspiration, feeds like a cancer on a man's self-respect, and degrades him in the estimation of men. It were better to die the possessor of a fearless spirit than to live a coward.

Among old England's heroic records there stands a dishonored name. One of her admirals, commanding a powerful fleet, met an enemy with a somewhat superior force. Doubting his competency to win a victory, and fearing defeat, that timid admiral refused a proffered opportunity to closely engage his foe. He did not fly. He did not decline to receive an attack. But he did not energetically throw himself on his adversary, who, equally timid, finally sailed away. This timidity, so unwonted in an English admiral, so unlike the heroic spirit of his race, roused a nation's wrath, and Admiral Byng perished on the scaffold!

In contrast with this timid man, see the brave commander of a little army sent against the best fortified city on the American continent. This city stood on the summit of a high, precipitous bank, which rose abruptly from a swiftly flowing river. Its ample fortifications were well manned and armed. Many bold men deemed its conquest impossible. But the daring spirit of a WOLFE conceived that everything is possible to him who has courage to attempt it with adequate means. He resolved to try. Landing his troops silently in the dead of night, he led them up, by paths that seemed impracticable, to some heights which commanded the city. When morning dawned his astonished adversary found himself compelled to fight or surrender. He fought and was conquered. The heroic Wolfe, while suffering mortal pain from a musket ball which had pierced his breast, heard a man shout, "They fly! they fly!"

"Who fly?" he asked.

"The French!" replied the voice.

"Thank God! I die happy," he cried, and closed his eyes in death.

These illustrations of a fearful and a heroic spirit may be regarded as representative facts. They should teach you to listen to the courageous rather than to the timid instincts of your nature in considering the difficulties which may confront you as you enter on a religious life. If you are governed by fear of persecution, of sacrifices, of trials, or of your own powers of perseverance, like Admiral Byng, you will meet with failure, disgrace, and death. If, like the undaunted Wolfe, you look defiantly at difficulties and resolve to conquer them, you will, like him, win victory and honorable renown. But with this significant difference: Byng's failure and Wolfe's victory reached only to the human and the mortal. If you fail you lose yourself and heaven; if you try and conquer you win immortal honor, with unmeasured, unending bliss.

Will you, then, refrain from seeking the Christian life through coward fear? Shall frowns, harsh words, cynical sneers, and apprehended trials of feeling frighten you from the gateway of the pleasant life? Are such fears manly? Are they worthy of your high capacities? Rather, do you not despise yourself for submitting, like a crouching slave, to their dictation? Rise, then, my young friend! Assert the dignity of your manhood! Listen to your soul's heroic voices. In the strife of the spiritual battle-field, be a Wolfe in daring, and you shall become a saint by winning the victory.

The puny rain-drop assaults the sturdy granite. Gliding into a slight fracture it invites the aid of frost and heat until, by expanding, it splits the rock asunder. In like manner do daring souls subdue mountains of opposition. In fact, opposition grappled is half overcome, and few Christians have found the actual trials of their early spiritual career half as terrible as their anticipations painted them. Even that most dreaded evil, persecution from our dearest friends, is usually found to lose half its fierceness when met in the spirit of meek decision. If you have an impenitent and persecuting father or mother, whose dreaded frowns keep you from coming to Christ, the following fact may encourage you.

"If you go again to hear such preachers I will turn you out of doors, sir!" said a stern father, one day, to his son who had become awakened under the preaching of an evangelical minister.

The young man trembled, for he knew his father was capable, if roused, of becoming a man of iron.

Yet so powerful were his convictions that he was led, in spite of his fears, to seek Christ in the prohibited church. A singular scene occurred there. The troubled manner of the youth arrested the eye of the preacher, and turning to a member of his Church he said:

"Brother! do you repent of coming to Christ?"

"No, sir," replied the man firmly, "I never was happy till I came. I only repent that I did not come to him sooner."

The minister then turned to a venerable father in his Church, and said: "Brother, do *you* repent of coming to Christ?"

"No, sir," the old man replied, "I have known the Lord from my youth upward."

The preacher now fixed his eye on the young man, and in tones of great tenderness said:

"Young man, are you willing to come to Christ?"

Finding himself thus made the object of universal attention, the young man bowed his head. At length, encouraged by the whispers of a Christian brother, he arose and said in a voice tremulous with emotion:

"Yes, sir?"

"But *when?*" asked the minister very solemnly.

"*Now*, sir!" replied the young man, with a firmness of tone that showed the irrevocable decision which his soul had made.

Having taken this stand he was afraid to meet his father. With a bursting heart he told the minister that the purpose he had formed made him homeless. "Fear not," the good man replied, soothingly; "I will write your father a letter; perhaps the spirit of God will lead him to a better mind."

The letter was written and sent. It calmed the tempest in the father's soul. He tolerated his son's presence. He took his wife and went to hear the Gospel for himself. It subdued him. It converted his wife also, and that young man, instead of becoming homeless, found his home more loving and blissful than it had ever been before. The cloud which lowered so terribly over him was big, not with storms of rage, but with dew-drops of sweetest blessing.

Here is another fact to the same point. A young lady being powerfully awakened, took her seat with a band of inquiring souls as a seeker of religion. The next day her betrothed met her and said:

"Well, Mary, I understand you have become a Methodist."

"No," she replied, "I am not a Methodist, but I am endeavoring to become a Christian."

"Well," said her intended, speaking in a pert tone, "if you are going to be a Methodist it is time for you and me to part."

"Very well," rejoined the lady with great firmness, "just as you please; good evening, sir!" and bowing gracefully to him, she walked to church. There she again took her seat with other penitent souls; and there the presence of a pardoning God filled her heart, and amply compensated her for the sacrifice she had made. But how great was her joy, on rising from her knees, to see her betrothed kneeling humbly at the altar. Her decision had startled him into concern for his own soul's welfare. By consenting to sacrifice her heart's most precious earthly affection, she gained the love of heaven and won back her earthly lover, not as she had surrendered him, but elevated into the highest style of man.

It may be thus with your apprehended difficulties, dear reader. God is able to bring water from the rock to quench your thirst. He can command the waters of the river to stand up in heaps to give you passage. He can throw down the mightiest walls in leading you on to victory. Therefore fear not, young seeker after Christ. God, even the God you desire to know, speaks these words to thee: "*Say to them that are of a fearful heart, Be strong, fear not: behold your God will come with vengeance, even God with a recompense:* HE WILL COME AND SAVE YOU!"

It sometimes pleases God to let the rage of the wicked burn like a flame of fire around those who seek his face. In times of open persecution, to profess Christ was to invoke the pains and penalties of martyrdom, and not unfrequently did the new-born believer find his worst foes in his own household. It must have been a fearful trial indeed, for the child to hear himself denounced at a heathen or an inquisitorial tribunal by his own father, and to be condemned to death on the testimony of her who bore him. Such opposition as this you cannot suffer. It is not permitted in these happier times. But what if it did await you? Would you be justified in refusing to come to Christ, even if your parents were certain to drag you from the seat of the penitent to the pyre of martyrdom with their own hands? Even in such a sad extremity of trial, would it not still be your duty to crush the fear of man in the dust, and boldly approach the cross, treading the path of blood? Should you shrink from such a fiery trial, would not the voice of Christ justly reprove you, saying: "He that loveth father or mother more than me is not worthy of me?"

How then can you dare to excuse yourself for staying away from Christ because of the comparatively trifling opposition which frowns upon you? Ought you not to fear the anger of God rather than that of man? "*Fear ye not me? saith the Lord. Will ye not tremble at my presence* which have placed the sand for the bound of the sea, by a perpetual decree, that it cannot pass it: and though the waves toss themselves, yet can they not prevail; though they roar yet can they not pass over it?" Consider this question, timid youth, and teach your fears wisdom by weighing well this further counsel of your neglected Saviour: "*Fear not them that kill the body, but are not able to kill the soul; but rather fear him which, after he hath killed, hath power to cast into hell; yea, I say unto you,* FEAR HIM!"

It may be that you are a son or daughter of mirth. You love gayety. Your language, if a young lady, is, "I can't give up my amusements. I belong to a select circle of merry associates. We have delightful sociables, private balls, and we often make up a splendid party to the opera or theater. Besides, I am passionately fond of novel reading. I can't give up these pleasures, and therefore 'I pray thee have me excused.'"

Perhaps the reader is a young man, and his plea is: "I belong to a club. Our meetings are occasions of rare jollity. We often take jaunts into the country, at which we joke, we sing, we dance, we drink. Indeed, we keep up a constant round of pleasures, which I can't give up for the sake of religion, and therefore 'I pray thee have me excused.'"

Possibly, however, a young man looks on these pages who makes no verbal plea. He dare not frame his excuse into words, but his will is bound to a life of sin by the chain of some criminal habit. Often, under the shadows of night, he creeps to some haunt of infamy, to indulge his excited passions in acts forbidden by God and by public sentiment. Though outwardly demure he is secretly a profligate, a gambler, a slave of her whose feet take hold of death. His darling vice controls his passions. He is a bird feeding greedily within the meshes of a fowler's net, and while he gives no verbal reason for his plea, he also says, "I pray thee have me excused."

To these and all others who prefer their fleshly and worldly lusts to God, I commend the following fact:

A lady was once talking eloquently in favor of theatrical performances. "They afford me three distinct pleasures," she remarked; "the pleasure of anticipation, the pleasure of beholding them, and the pleasure of reflecting upon them afterward."

"Pardon me, madam," said a clergyman, who heard her remark, "but you have forgotten to name a fourth pleasure afforded by the theater."

"Indeed, sir!" she replied, "what can that be?"

Looking solemnly at her the clergyman gravely said: "The pleasure of reflecting upon it in the hour of death!"

The lady started as if a serpent had stung her. She felt that her favorite amusement would not afford material for agreeable reflection on a death-bed. With true wisdom she concluded that pleasures which would not bear to be reflected on in the hour of death were not fit to be indulged in during life, and acting upon this conviction, she exchanged the pleasures of sin for the richer delights of the pleasant way. Would that my reader could be persuaded to imitate her example.

I have read of monarchs who lost their kingdoms by abandoning themselves to the lusts of the flesh; of men who to gratify their passion for gambling have beggared themselves, and, at least in legends, of others who, for greed of gold, ambition, or pleasure, have bargained their souls to Satan. In all such cases the folly of the parties is painfully preposterous. But is the folly of my reader less? They were foolish because they gave property, life, soul, for such paltry considerations. They sold the valuable for the valueless, the precious for the vile. Does not the reader do the same? For trifling indulgences, for a few years of unsatisfying pleasures, for really less of this life than religion would give him, he rejects the smile of God, the lofty enjoyments of Divine communion, and the felicities of eternal life. He sacrifices heaven at the shrine of earth; he gives the infinite for the finite; the eternal for the momentary and perishing. This is folly's climax. This is a deed at which heaven itself is astonished, and in presence of which even God himself exclaims: "Be astonished, O ye heavens, at this, and be horribly afraid; be ye very desolate, saith the Lord, for my people have committed two evils; they have forsaken me the fountain of living waters, and hewed them out cisterns, broken cisterns, that can hold no water"

God sometimes deals in a very summary manner with such as you, my pleasure-loving reader. Here is an example.

A young lady of fifteen was deeply convicted. She resisted the Spirit and lost her religious feelings in the pursuits of worldly pleasure. When eighteen her convictions returned. They were more powerful than before. Her pastor urged her to decide for Christ, but to all his entreaties she replied:

"I can't be a Christian *now*."

Speaking of this reply to a female friend, she said: "I would have yielded to my convictions, only I had engaged to attend a ball on the coming fourth of July."

Disappointed girl! On the day of that fatal ball she followed the corpse of her father to the tomb! A few weeks later she too became the victim of death. She died without hope or feeling. She sold her soul for a ball, but lost the paltry price, although she paid the terrible forfeit.

If you are a candidate for the rewards of mammon, and excuse yourself because you wish to devote yourself to money-making, you are exposed to the same censures and dangers as the children of mirth. When you lift up your eyes in hell, and see heaven afar off, the thought, "I sold that infinite bliss for base gold," will torment your soul with inconceivable pain. Remember, "Treasures of wickedness profit nothing; but righteousness delivereth from death."

It may be that none of these things lie at the basis of your excuse, but your heart whispers, "*I am afraid I shall not obtain religion if I seek it, and then I shall be laughed at; or, if I should find it, I should not be able to hold out; and therefore I pray thee have me excused.*"

If, precious youth, you had to meet an unwillingness in God to save you, there would be some grounds for your fear. But mark! God is seeking to save you. He wills your salvation. He is "*not willing that any should perish, but that all should come to repentance.*" Christ has died for you. The Holy Spirit convinces you of sin and strives to conduct you to the cross. Millions, just such as you are, have sought and found mercy. God's faithfulness to his word of promise has never been broken. No, not in a single instance. The way to the Saviour is so straight and plain that even little children can find him. Your failure is therefore impossible *if you are in earnest;* for "WHOSOEVER WILL" may come and partake of the water of life freely. Blessed be God!

When ALEXANDER THE GREAT was assaulting a city in India, he was the first to scale the walls. Four of his officers joined him, when the scaling-ladder broke and the monarch stood almost alone, exposed to all the fury of his enemies. What could he do? Leap back to his army below? That would turn them backward and lose the city. What then? Why, leap into the midst of his foes, trust to his good sword, and bide the help of his troops. He did so, placing his back against the wall of the fort and fighting with heroic courage until his soldiers came to his rescue and victory crowned his banners.

Now, if you will throw yourself into the work of seeking God with the resolute spirit of this warrior-king, there is no possibility of your failure to find his mercy; and if, with equal resolution, you pursue your way, after being pardoned, there is little probability of your apostasy. God seeketh you! God will help you! Be in earnest, and you will be saved; for "EVERY ONE that asketh receiveth; and he that seeketh findeth; and to him that knocketh it shall be opened."

Away then, beloved youth, with all your wicked excuses. They are all the language of sinful disinclination. They are all lighter than the froth of the sea, baseless as the fabric of a vision, unreasonable as folly's idlest blab. Away with them. Drag your reluctant spirit to the feet of Christ. Struggle against your own disinclination. Read the word of God faithfully. Cry out against yourself in the ear of the Almighty. Turn your face toward him, resolving if you perish to do so at his feet crying for mercy, and, believe me, no soul can perish there!

CHAPTER X.

THE PROCRASTINATOR'S DOOM.

IMAGINE yourself the inmate of a cell in some great prison. See a small tank suspended in a corner, with its top so close to the ceiling that you cannot look upon its contents. An unseen pipe conducts water to it in single drops. Suppose that you are under sentence of death, and that you are to be led out to die the moment after the first drop of water overflows the tank and falls upon the prison-floor! Would you not tremble as you heard the unceasing pat, pat, pat, of those terrible water-drops falling day and night? While you slept and while you were awake, while you ate and while you drank, ever and always they would keep dropping, slowly but surely filling up the fatal cistern, and bringing on the dreadful moment in which the signal-drop would flow over the edge, roll down the side, and fall with a death-dealing splash upon the floor of your cell. Such an imprisonment and such a doom are too painful to dwell upon.

And yet, beloved youth, this terrible picture is but a dim image of your actual relations to God and eternity. Your immortal soul is imprisoned in its cell of clay, and is under sentence of eternal death. True, that sentence is held in suspension to give you opportunity either to seek its reversal and be saved, or "to fill up the measure of your iniquities" and be damned. Every moment of your life spent in alienation from God adds a drop to the already large amount of your transgression, and contributes to fill up the "measure of your iniquities." When that is accomplished you will be eternally ruined. The Spirit will forsake you, the god of this world will bind you with chains of steel to the death-cart, and when Divine Justice gives the signal, will drive you forth and cast you into the bottomless pit. "Every tree that bringeth not forth good fruit is hewn down and cast into the fire."

How full of real terror, therefore, is your present condition, would you but open your eyes and unseal your ears! Would you reflect, every act of sin, every moment's neglect to come to Jesus, would sound like the drop of water in your prison's tank, and you would tremble, lest, the "measure of your iniquities" being filled, the Spirit of grace should forsake you and seal you over to "hardness of heart and blindness of mind" for evermore. Pause, therefore, beloved youth. Add not another sin to that fatal measure. Say not, "I will seek Christ by and by, but not now." Tarry not in the way of the procrastinator, for danger and death lurk there like robbers lying in wait for the unwary traveler.

When the ROMANS sought occasion to begin the second Punic war, they sent embassadors to state their demands to the Carthaginian Senate. The reply of that body not being satisfactory, one of the Romans took up the folded lappet of his robe, and said, in a haughty tone:

"I bring here either peace or war, the choice is left to yourselves!"

"And we leave the choice to you," replied the Senate.

"I give you war, then," said the Roman, unfolding his robe as he spoke.

"And we as heartily accept it," retorted the senators of Carthage, in tones as haughty as those of the Roman.

I presume, my reader, you shrink from giving utterance to such daring words as fell from the lips of the men of Carthage, when the demands of Jehovah are pressed upon you by his embassadors. Like the Roman deputies, they bring you the alternative of peace or war, life or death; *the choice is left to you.* In your case, however, God prefers peace between you and himself. He desires you to choose life, because he is "not willing that any should perish, but that all should come to repentance." Still, the choice is left to you. It has been pressed upon you for years. It is urged upon you now. Since your first hour of accountability, the Holy Ghost has stood before you constantly, saying: "If it seem evil unto you to serve the Lord, choose you *this day* whom ye will serve:" "Behold, *now* is the accepted time; behold, *now* is the day of salvation!"

Have you met this demand in a brave, manly manner? Like the men of Carthage, have you spoken your mind freely, and, in the language of the husbandman's son, said to your Maker, "*I will not* serve thee?" No, you have not had the hardihood to rush with such a daring answer on the sword of his anger. But you have used crafty words, saying, "I will serve thee, Lord, but not now. I will seek thy face, but not to-day. In some future hour of convenience I will make my peace with thee: for the present I must enjoy the profits and the pleasures of sin."

Foolish youth! can you imagine that God is deceived by such silly craftiness as this? Does he not look with searching eye into your heart and see the cowardice which begot those words of procrastination? Does he not know that but for your indestructible consciousness of his power to cast you into hell, your reply to him would be as haughty, as decided, as daring as that of the senators of Carthage to the Roman deputy? Does he not also know that your words are equivalent to an absolute rejection of his service? What have you to do with *to-morrow?* Is not your life a passing cloud, an exhaling dew-drop, a fading flower? Knowing this, he does not ask you what you will do *to-morrow.* His inquiry is, Will you serve me *to-day?* And when you reply in words of procrastination, you do in effect meet the Divine demand with a positive refusal. It is the same as if you said, "I will not!"

O how wicked it is to procrastinate! Aversion, cowardice, falsehood, rebellion, ingratitude, and folly are all included in it. Moreover, it is a sin which proclaims its own abominable wickedness. Why do you, young procrastinator, only *defer* instead of absolutely declining the service of God? Is not your promise of future obedience an admission of his eternal right to claim all the service you are able to give, and of your obligations to render it? You know it is so. You also know that your promise to give him your heart "by and by" is a miserable, cowardly subterfuge, by which you secretly flatter yourself he will be so propitiated as to wink at your present wicked rejection of his love. Hence, your purpose to serve God in the future stamps the brand of deliberate wickedness on your present conduct. It is a proclamation to men, angels, and devils, by which you declare that, although you know it is your duty to give your heart to Christ, yet you are determined to trample upon his claims and your own obligations, and to spend the choicest portion of your life in sinning against the love which bought your pardon with the blood of the only begotten Son!

This *is* wickedness indeed—open, unblushing, conscious, contemptuous, dastardly wickedness! The immoralities of an ignorant heathen, or papist, are venial when compared with the sin of procrastination in one whose path, from the cradle to this solemn hour, has been radiant with beams of light and love from the Sun of righteousness, and overhung with the richly laden branches of the tree of life. It is of itself sufficient to justify your being driven into everlasting banishment from the "presence of God and the glory of his power." It is a sin by which you tread "under foot the Son of God," count "the blood of the covenant an unholy thing," and do "despite unto the Spirit of grace!" Believe me, procrastination is a deadly sin.

It is also as *dangerous* as it is abominable. Perhaps there is no other sin so successful in beguiling hearers of the Gospel into perdition, as procrastination. Hell is crowded with its victims, and millions of living youth, now walking in the road to destruction, are kept there by its necromantic spells.

In Spenser's "Faerie Queen," the Redcross Knight, enthralled by the blandishments of the false Duessa, is led into the wooded domain of a savage giant. Seeking repose beneath the shade of the forest trees he finds a fountain,

"Where bubbling wave did ever freshly well."

Ignorant of its qualities he quaffs its crystal waters, when,

> "Eftsoones his manly forces 'gan to fayle,
> And mightie strong was turned to feeble frayle."

While the knight is weak from the effects of these enchanted waters, the giant comes forth, "hideous, horrible, and high," and challenges him to battle. But the poor knight, "faint in every joint and vein," is no match for such a foe. After a feeble defense he falls before the giant's might, and is borne with "hasty force" to the castle of his conqueror, and thrown, "without remorse," into a "dungeon deep."

This romantic fancy of the poet aptly illustrates one of the evil influences of procrastination. As that enchanted fount enervated the Redcross knight, so does procrastination narcotize your conscience and make your will "feeble frayle." For proof of this, consult your own experience. When your moral nature is aroused by the voices of truth, how do you manage to lull it to slumber? Do you not do it by drinking of the waters of procrastination? "By and by I will seek the Lord," you say, and forthwith your conscience is overcome by the lassitude of sleep, and then you are "led captive by the devil at his will." Is it not so? And is it not equally true, that your habit of procrastination has reduced your conscience to such an habitually slumberous condition that it rarely utters its protests against your life of sinful pleasure and wicked unbelief? You know this is its state; and it being so, are you not in danger of sinking into a state of absolute moral insensibility? Then you will cease to have even the *fear* of God before your eyes. Then what will become of your oft-repeated promise to serve God? Will you not be likely to despise it and to die impenitent?

See that bright-eyed maiden, seated on the green bank of yonder running stream. Her heart is gay, and her hands are filled with flowers of beauty rare. Full of sportive feeling she casts a flower into the stream, claps her little white hands, and smiles to see it float away upon the sunlit water. One by one she throws her flowers away, until the last is gone. And now she weeps, wishes she had kept them, and vainly cries to the unconscious stream, "Give me back my flowers!"

In this maiden's folly you may see another evil influence of procrastination. It is beguiling you of your time as the stream beguiled the child of her flowers. *Hours* are precious opportunities, especially those sacred ones in which serious thoughts give birth to anxious questionings about the soul. Such hours are worth more than rubies. They are the golden periods of the "accepted time." If properly employed they would yield you eternal salvation. But every act of procrastination casts one of them into the stream of time. Having flung away one such priceless opportunity by delay, it is easy to throw away a second, and easier still to waste a third. Repeating these acts creates a habit by force of which the mind comes at last to spontaneously, almost unconsciously, postpone its religious duties as regularly as they are presented to it. As a consequence the original promise to seek God is not kept. The "convenient time"—the imaginary "by and by"—never arrives, for before it comes the procrastinator is surprised by the summons of death, and drops, with his violated promises, into the lake of everlasting damnation. As saith the poet:

> "The hoary fool, who many days
> Has struggled with continued sorrow,
> Renews his hope, and fondly lays
> The desperate bet upon to-morrow.

"To-morrow comes! 'Tis noon; 'tis night!
This day like all the former flies;
Yet on he goes to seek delight
To-morrow, when to-night he dies!"

"He that, being often reproved, hardeneth his neck, shall suddenly be destroyed, and that without remedy."

Suddenly destroyed! What a fearful thought! After so many day-dreams of prospective godliness, to be suddenly driven into hell is a sad close to a life so full of hopeful beginnings as yours. Yet God has spoken it. Sudden destruction is your doom if you continue to "harden your neck" by delaying your duty. You may see how God often treats such as you are in the following facts:

Three young men, with axes on their shoulders, were on their way to the woods one morning, when they met a minister who spoke earnest words to them on the subject of their salvation. Two of them listened seriously; the third pointed, with gayety in his manner, to a distant house and said:

"Do you see that splendid white house on yonder farm?"

"Yes."

"Well, sir, that estate has been willed to me by

my uncle. There are incumbrances upon it which I must remove before the farm can be fully mine. As soon as I have paid them all off I mean to become a Christian."

The minister sighed, looked affectionately at the youth, and replied: "Ah, young man, beware! You may never see that day. While you are gaining the world you may lose your soul!"

"*I'll run the risk!*" rejoined the confident heir.

They parted. The minister went his way seeking other souls for his Lord. The young men entered the woodlands and began chopping. The ax of the young heir cut deeply into an old tree with swift repeated strokes. He saw not a huge dead branch which trembled above him as his sturdy blows fell on the trunk beneath. But the jar of his ax shook it off, and it fell with a fearful crash upon his head, and stretched him dead upon the ground! He was "*suddenly destroyed, and that without remedy!*"

Take another fact. A young lady joined the Sabbath school in a church of which I was pastor at the time. The teacher, who was very pious, spoke to her concerning her soul. "Time enough yet," said the girl, laughing, "I am only sixteen years old. I mean to enjoy the world a year or two before I seek religion."

Two weeks from the hour in which she gave utterance to those idle words, I stood beside her corpse exhorting a crowded audience to beware how, like her, they postponed until to-morrow the work God required them to perform to-day. She, too, was "*suddenly destroyed.*"

God is in earnest with you, young immortal, and he wishes you to be in earnest with him. His rights over you, his mercies to you, his great gift of his Son's life, are objects of infinite importance to him. He will not permit you to trifle with them with impunity. Yet, what is procrastination but a wicked trifling with these solemn realities? What deliberate contempt you pour on the smile of God, on the blood of Jesus, on the Holy Spirit, when you coolly bid them stand aside until you are at leisure to accept them? *You* postpone *his* offer of love and mercy! Think of it. *You*, a mere moth whom he could destroy with a glance of his eye, postpone the acceptance of the Almighty's richest gift. *You*, a ruined sinner, defer acceptance of that loving help without which you must be endlessly wretched. What insensate pride! What unparalleled madness! Surely if God's patience were not infinite, he would smite you with sudden destruction for daring to insult him by postponing your acceptance of the great salvation. But, blessed be his holy name! he is very long-suffering, and therefore he endures much from you.

Still it is dangerous to trifle with this gracious long-suffering. Deep as it is, it may be sounded with the line of willful presumption. The ancient Jews did this, and God swore in his wrath: "They shall not enter into my rest." The burial of a whole generation in the sands of the desert testified Jehovah's faithfulness to that terrible oath. "Wherefore, as the Holy Ghost saith, To-day if *ye* will hear his voice harden not *your* heart." Nothing grieves and angers your Creator more than the presumptuous trifling which is involved in the habit of procrastination. Listen to the hoarse voice of your insulted God and tremble. He says:

"Because I have called and ye refused;... ye have set at naught all my counsel, and would none of my reproof: I also will laugh at your calamity: I will mock when your fear cometh."

I will laugh at your calamity! Awful words, pregnant with manifold horrors! *Your calamity!* What will that be? What, but a heart forsaken of God, blinded by the "god of this world," given over to hardness and unbelief, abandoned by the Holy Spirit, damned this side of the grave? And when you have brought this "calamity" upon yourself, He with whom you have so long trifled will pity no more, but he will "*laugh!*" When your "fear cometh," as come it must, he will not fly to your relief but will "MOCK!" because you "did not choose the fear of the Lord."

Beware then, thou child of many prayers, how you tempt God to bring this calamity upon you by the withdrawal of his Holy Spirit. Has he not said, "Grieve not the Holy Spirit!" "Quench not the Spirit!" "If ye seek him he will be found of you; but if ye forsake him, he will forsake you." I cannot tell you when, at what age, or by what particular act the Spirit is quenched; but, remember,

> "There is a time, we know not when,
> A point we know not where,
> That marks the destiny of men
> To glory or despair."

That you may feel these threats of spiritual abandonment are more than empty sounds, I will sketch a fact or two, from among thousands of similar cases, in which persons have been awfully conscious of having crossed the line of doom.

"Have you never felt concern for your soul, madam?" said a minister to a lady who was about thirty years old.

"Yes," she replied, "*I think that few have felt as I did once.*"

"At what period of life, madam?"

"When I was about fifteen," said she, "I felt myself a sinner. I could not sleep. For three years I seldom had peace a week at a time. I knew the Spirit was striving with me and that I ought to yield. But I loved the pleasures of youth. I banished thoughts of eternity. I read novels and romances, which gave me relief awhile, but my distress returned. At last I went to the ball-room, and *I have never had religious feelings since!*"

The minister sighed, and asked, "Have you no fears lest you have grieved away the Holy Spirit?"

"*I have no doubt of it*, and I shall be lost," said the lady, with the utmost coolness.

The good minister was profoundly moved. He pleaded with earnest words and sympathetic tears, begging her to try the effect of prayer. Vain attempt! She arose, waved her hand, and as she retired from the room, said:

"All this has been tried upon me before. Nothing that you or any other man can say on that subject can move me now. MY DOOM IS FIXED!"

Let me pencil another illustration. An impenitent old man was asked, "Did you ever feel the importance of religion?"

"Yes, when I was young I often had serious times," he said.

"When did you feel most?"

"When I was seventeen I felt deeply, at times, and for two or three years after. I resolved, however, to put it off until I was settled in life. After I was married I again felt that I ought then to begin my religious life. But I had bought a farm, and I thought, as it would cost time and money to attend church, I would save the expense until I paid for my farm. I resolved to put off being a Christian for ten years. The ten years passed, but I thought no more about it.

I often try to think now, but *cannot keep my mind on the subject one moment!*"

"Try, do try, my friend," entreated the minister, "for God is gracious."

"It is too late," said the gray-headed patriarch; "*I believe my doom is sealed*, and it is just it should be so, for the Spirit strove long with me, but I refused."

Reader, can you endure the thought of becoming so petrified in heart as to be "past feeling," like this man and that lady? You cannot, I know. The bare idea quickens your heart-throbs. You shrink before it as from the brink of a frightful gulf. It is well you have such feelings; but remember that every purpose of delay, every excuse offered, every mental act of resistance to the Spirit, is a step toward their doom. I do not affirm that without *instant* repentance you will *certainly* enter the iron cage of stern despair in which they were shut up, for you *may* find the wicket-gate hereafter. But fail not to consider that you are in the very path by which they walked into that cage! Is not that fact conclusive proof of your danger? Should it not be to you as the angel in the way of Balaam? Heed it, study it, be moved by it, and rest not until, like Bunyan's pilgrim, you turn your back upon a sinful life, and, with God's book in your hand, are found in the way to the celestial city. O hasten, hasten, young sinner,

"Hasten, mercy to implore!
Stay not for the morrow's sun,
Lest thy season should be o'er
Ere this evening's stage be run."

Sometimes the Spirit remains with the stubborn procrastinator to show him his guilt, but not to light his wayward feet to the cross. The following examples are in point.

A gay young man, charmed by the voices of sinful pleasures, threw away his hours of opportunity, silencing the reproofs of his faithful conscience by promises of what he would do by and by. In the heyday of his delights a mortal disease took possession of the chamber of life and bade him depart quickly to the realms of death. He shuddered at the thought of meeting his neglected Creator. A friend pointed him to the cross of Jesus, saying:

"Look to Christ. His promises of mercy are very precious. His Gospel is a balm for all the wounds which sin has made in your soul."

With despair in his flashing eyes, and agony in his hollow voice, the youth replied:

"True, but that Gospel which *I have despised through my life* AFFORDS ME NO BALM IN MY DEATH. There is no mercy for me now!"

Having spoken thus, he closed his eyes and shortly afterward expired. Procrastination had robbed him of eternal life.

Three students, high in spirits and vigorous of limb, were bathing in a river at a small distance above its falls. After swimming for a while, they agreed to float down the stream. The calmly flowing waters bore them gently along, until, having approached the falls, the students felt that the velocity of the current was increasing rapidly. Two of them, feeling alarmed, swam at once for the shore, from which they hailed their companion, and begged him not to risk his life by floating any farther. But he only laughed and said, "It is pleasant floating."

Then his companions, trembling at his fool-hardiness, shouted:

"Make for the shore, or you will go over the falls."

Again he laughed, and replied, "It is pleasant floating."

A moment more, and he felt the current sweeping him along with alarming swiftness. Then he was terrified, and with strong efforts tried to swim ashore. O how he struggled against that remorseless stream. Vain attempt! The roaring waters mocked his anguish, drowned his cries, and hurried him to his fate. Soon, alas! how soon, he reached the awful brink. Then, throwing out his arms, he leaped up, uttered a piercing shriek, and was dragged by the mighty arms of the flood down into the boiling abyss below.

Mournful spectacle! And yet is it not a picture of the manner in which a class of procrastinators reach their doom? *It is pleasant floating*, said that ill-fated youth, thinking he would swim away from the falls when the danger became imminent. *It is pleasant sinning*, cries the procrastinator, to the friends of his soul, who vainly try to call him from the brink of the pit; and he too thinks he will stop sinning in time to be saved; yes, *it is pleasant sinning* when the voices of the Spirit are lost in the noises of dissipation, and the drugged conscience slumbers in some out-of-the-way corner of the soul. But is not the awakening terrible when the roaring waters warn the unhappy child of delay that he is on the brink of that mysterious gulf we call eternity? What alarm startles him then! What horror thrills him! What shrinking! What struggling! What a vain leaping back from destiny! What overwhelming ruin closes his career! The following facts are in point:

A pastor once besought one of his regular hearers to seek a personal interest in Christ. With a laugh upon her lips, she replied:

"*O, I shall only want five minutes when I am dying to cry for mercy*, and I have no doubt God Almighty will give it me."

With tearful eyes and earnest words that pastor besought the infatuated woman not to presume so daringly on the forbearance of God. Again and again he urged her to immediate repentance; again and again she repeated her presumptuous words. Her heart was hardened against God. Mark the result.

One day, as the pastor was walking down the street, a young woman, greatly excited, ran up to him and exclaimed:

"O Mr. East, I have found you! Do come to my mother, sir! Come this minute, sir! She is dying!"

With rapid steps the good man followed the agitated girl. Judge his surprise when he entered the death-chamber and the agonized features of the presumptuous procrastinator, with whom he had so vainly labored, met his eye! She was at the point of death. Turning her expiring eyes upon her pastor, she cried out in piercing tones:

"O Mr. East, I am damned! I am damned!"

Horror-struck, the good pastor stepped to her bedside with words of mercy on his lips. But it was too late. Her spirit was struggling in the abysmal depths of infinite despair!

Now let me lead you into an old Moorish-looking stone building in the town of Monterey. Open the door gently, for see! on that little cot lies a young lieutenant in the American army. He is sick, very sick. A military friend is bending over his feverish body. Hark! they are talking. Let us listen.

"How do you feel to-night?" asks the soldier in a whisper.

The sick man stares vacantly at the questioner. Now he speaks: "I must die—*die*—yes DIE, and see my home no more!"

He pauses again, but soon speaks in a louder voice: "But the past! the future! The *past!* a scene of hardship and toil—a jealous striving to be great; a mere vacuum, void of everything save conscience. The *future!* ah, the terrible future! Hope? *hope* is extinct. I am irretrievably lost—a curse to existence, a miserable, degraded wretch!"

Now he is silent. The cemetery clock strikes eleven! The dying soldier speaks again: "What!" he exclaims, "has the clock tolled another hour and still I exist? O that I had never had a being!"

See him stretch out his arms as if reaching after something. Hear him cry, "Mother! mother! save me! save your son!"

He is quiet again and gazes into vacuity. Once more he cries: "Come back! come back!—but no, she has left me."

His strength is gone. He falls back upon his couch. An hour passes. He slowly articulates, "God—is—just!" and as the church-bell tolls the midnight hour his soul passes into eternity.

Such is the doom of the procrastinator. A death full of anguish, or a heart forsaken of God, and therefore hard as granite, is his lot. In either case a heritage of endless calamity is his destiny. Reader, do you wish to sink beneath such a weary weight of woe? Are you prepared to be abandoned of God? If not, then, by all that is terrible in the thought, delay not another moment the duty which ought to have been done years ago. Now, before you lay aside this book, record your solemn purpose to "flee from the wrath to come." Resolve, O resolve to turn at once from sin to God. Jesus calls thee. Hark!

> "Jesus knocketh at thy heart,
> Rise and let him in;
> Knocketh with a bleeding hand,
> Wounded for thy sin.
> Jesus knocketh night and day,
> Waiting at thy side;
> Canst thou turn the Lord away?
> Scorn the Crucified?"

Jesus loves you! Did he not shed his blood because of the love he bore you? Has he not wept over you, interceded for you, striven with you, done all that infinite love guided by wisdom could devise to save you? Could he have done more than he has done? Why then will you longer refuse to give him your heart?

Jesus seeks you! Never did shepherd seek a lost sheep as faithfully as Jesus has sought to win your soul to his service. Do you remember those loving thoughts of God, those solemn melting moods of mind, those tears of transient penitence, those breathings of desire, those inward warnings which have so often come upon you ever since the days of your childhood? They were the whispers, the motions, the breathings of Jesus. He was seeking thee. He seeks thee now. Will you bid him go empty away?

Why will you destroy yourself? Can you endure everlasting burnings? Can you afford to lose the joys of religion here and of heaven hereafter? Is there any wisdom or any profit in staying away from Christ? Do not your reason and conscience tell you that you ought to seek God? Why then will you longer act in opposition to your profoundest convictions?

Why will you destroy others? You cannot go to hell alone. Your example is sure to lead some of your friends and companions along the path you choose. You have influence over some who are very dear to your affections. Will you expend it in promoting their misery? Will you lead your companions into hell? Will you diffuse the malaria of irreligion throughout the social atmosphere in which you live? O cruel youth, forbear! If you have no pity on yourself, pity your friends and spare them the misery of being damned through your influence and example! For the sake of others, if not for your own, I beseech you give your heart to Christ at once.

Do you wish to break the hearts of your pious mother and father? This question is for the child of pious parents. If, through procrastinating, you are "suddenly destroyed," or die either in the torpor or the agonies of despair, your spiritual destruction will bring the gray hairs of your parents in sorrow to the grave. Let me sketch a thrilling illustration for your consideration.

Yonder is an old man, gray-haired and feeble. His face is pale, big tears are trickling down his withered cheeks, and he is wringing his hands as if some sharp agony was wrestling with his spirit. What ails him?

He has heard that his son is in an adjacent mine in which a "sand-blast" has just been fired. "Cannot you leave your son in the hands of God?" inquires a friend.

"O!" said he, "I could if he had religion!"

There is now a stir about the mouth of the mine. A man is coming up the ladder with tidings of the old man's son. "Is he alive?" the people ask.

"No, his head is all torn to pieces!" is the terrible reply.

The old man's friend leads him back among the rocks and says: "My dear friend, you must give up your boy; he is dead!"

Fearful was the shriek which escaped that old man's lips, as still wringing his hands, he cried:

"O his poor soul! what has become of his soul?"

Who could sound the depths of that father's grief over the lost soul of his son? Who conceive the intensity of his agony? Yet thus will that noble father and that sweet mother of thine suffer if they should see you die an impenitent sinner. Do you wish to add the crime of breaking their hearts to your other sins? If not, I beseech you, humble yourself under the mighty hand of God this moment.

You are sure to be pardoned if you seek the Saviour. Encouraging thought! Having died as your substitute; having made every possible provision for your salvation; having invited you to his arms; having offered and promised you pardon; having made it the grand purpose of his government over you to bring you into union with himself, there is, there can be no doubt of your finding his favor if you will seek it heartily and at once. Listen! The Saviour speaks. He says: "Come unto me ALL ye that labor and are heavy laden, and I will give you rest." "The Spirit and the bride say, Come. And let him that heareth say, Come. And let *him that is athirst* come. And *whosoever will*, let him take the water of life freely."

Come then, beloved youth, come to thy long-neglected Saviour. Seek him now, just now. Say to him in all sincerity:

> "Here is my heart! My God, I give it thee:
> I heard thee call and say,
> 'Not to the world, my child, but unto me;'
> I heard, and will obey.
> Here is love's offering to my King,
> Which, a glad sacrifice, I bring—
> Here is my heart."

CHAPTER XI.

VOICES OF DUTY.

When the illustrious Nelson was leading England's proud fleet into action with the combined navies of France and Spain, he electrified his followers by signalizing, as his battle-cry, the following lofty sentiment: "England expects every man to do his duty!"

When the hero of Austerlitz wished to excite his victorious troops to fresh deeds of danger and daring, he thrilled them with this proclamation: "When everything necessary to the prosperity of our country is obtained, I will lead you back to France. My people will again behold you with joy. It will be enough for one of you to say, 'I was at the battle of Austerlitz!' for all your fellow-citizens to exclaim, 'There is a brave man!'"

You can doubtless see a wide difference between the signal of the admiral and the proclamation of the emperor. There is a touch of sublimity in both, because they both make each person addressed regard his personal conduct as the object of a nation's observation. But how superior is the signal to the proclamation, in the sentiment it addresses and the motive it evokes? The proclamation appeals to the *vanity* of the troops, by promising them the voices of national applause as the reward of their bravery; the signal speaks to the *patriotism and the moral sense* of the sailors, by suggesting consciousness of duty performed up to the height of the national expectation, as a motive to that heroic effort which conquers, or dies in the pursuit of victory.

Which, then, is the nobler appeal? If conscientious patriotism be a loftier sentiment than love of personal glory; if exalted motives gild the acts they inspire with their own peculiar luster, then is the signal as superior to the proclamation as the heroism of duty is to the achievments of vanity.

I have used these illustrations for the purpose of introducing a motive to godliness, which, while it underlies the preceding chapters, has not been made prominent in them—*the motive of duty?* Thus far I have chiefly exhibited piety as the only dispenser of true happiness. My appeal has mainly been to your self-love—not to your "private self-love," or *selfishness*, but to that regard for your own well-being which is natural, and which, if sought in harmony with the Divine will and the good of others, is right. Hitherto I have taken for granted that you admit a life of piety to be your duty; but now I wish to make this motive emphatic—to show you that religion is duty, that God has rights in you which you are bound to respect, and that the "LORD hath chosen you to stand before him, to serve him."

You have probably read an incident in the life of Prussia's most warlike sovereign, Frederick the Great, in which that strange monarch's will was successfully resisted by a sturdy miller. The uncouth edifice in which the latter ground corn for the citizens of Potsdam, obstructed the view from the windows of the royal palace. The king, annoyed by its presence, sent a messenger to its owner with the question:

"For what price will you sell your mill?"

"For no price," replied the independent miller, who, having received the estate from his ancestors had no wish to part with it.

The king, angered by this reply to his overture, said to his officers, "Let the mill be pulled down!"

When the servants of his majesty began the work of demolition the honest miller quietly folded his arms and said:

"The king may do this, but there are laws in Prussia."

This bold man, conscious of his rights, invoked the law. His cause was heard, and the court decided that the king should rebuild the mill, and pay the miller a large sum of money besides, as a compensation for the injury done to his business by the destruction of his property. The king's feelings were sorely wounded by this decision, but his sense of justice prevailed, and he submitted, saying:

"I am glad to find that just laws and upright judges exist in my kingdom."

In this interesting fact you cannot fail to see that the miller, being the legal owner of the mill, had the right to control it as he pleased. He could keep it, sell it, give it away, alter it, allow it to stand, or pull it down, and so long as he did not use it to the injury of his neighbors, no one, not even the king, had any right to interfere with the disposition he might choose to make of it. When, therefore, the king tried to compel him to sell it, and when he pulled it down, he wronged him, by trampling on his rights as its legal proprietor. Both as a man and a king he ought to have respected those rights. It was his duty to do so.

I have used this historic fact to impress you with the great truth that Jehovah, being the owner and proprietor of your nature, has the right to govern you in all things, and that you, being his creature—ay, his *property*—are bound by the solemn obligations of duty to dispose of yourself according to his will.

"Behold all souls are mine." "I am the Lord thy God." "Ye call me Master and Lord, and ye say well, for so I am." "God that made the world, and all things therein, seeing that he is Lord of heaven and earth, . . . commandeth all men everywhere to repent." In these words of the Most High he asserts his proprietorship of your soul. He claims to be your owner in the most absolute sense, founding his claim on the fact of his creatorship, which makes his rights of property in you most perfect and unimpeachable.

Let this thought sink into your mind, young

reader. God is your *owner*. He made you, and therefore you belong to him, mind and body, intellect, affections, will; every faculty, capacity, and power; everything within you and without you; all you see, hear, feel; all and everything belong to him in the most positive and absolute sense. What a perfect state of dependence is yours! "You are not your own," but God's; just as the earth, the sun, the moon, and the stars are his property, so are you!

If the miller's legal ownership in the mill at Potsdam gave him the right to control it, how much more does God's absolute ownership of your nature give him the right to govern you? You cannot deny his right, since every claim for your obedience which he sets up finds its justification in your reason, every command he utters from Sinai or Calvary has its echo in your own conscience.

If the miller's rights in his ancestral estate made it the duty of the Prussian king to leave him unmolested in disposing of it, how much more do God's rights of property in you make it your duty to use yourself according to his wishes? Rights and duties are reciprocal, you know. If it be God's *right* to control your person and direct your conduct, is it not also your *duty* to submit to his government? Appeal to your conscience! Bring the law of Horeb and the teachings of Calvary, in all the completeness and spirituality of their precepts, before it. Let them instruct you, undisturbed by the voices of passion, unblinded by the mists and vapors of carnal desires. Do they not compel you to say, in the most sacred sanctuary of your spirit: "I OUGHT to submit in all things and at all times to the commands of God?"

I know it is even so. Your reason and your conscience acknowledge both God's rights and your duty. While, therefore, you are moved to a life of piety by considerations of your personal well-being, let this be a corner-stone of your religious character—IT IS MY DUTY TO SERVE GOD! I WILL OBEY HIM BECAUSE I AM HIS CREATURE, AND HE IS MY GOD!

When King Frederick tore down the mill, did he not trample on the legal rights of the miller? When he took away its materials, was he not guilty of robbery? By disregarding the law did he not set an example which, if generally imitated, would have filled his kingdom with riot and anarchy? By what names, then, shall I designate your acts of disobedience to God? Does not every refusal of yours to obey him, trample upon his rights, rob him of that service from your powers which is his just due, and set an example of rebellion which, if universally followed by the sentient creation, would leave him without a rational worshiper in the universe? Yes, sin is rebellion, treason, robbery, injustice, wrong. It is the greatest injury you can do to yourself. It is base insult to the King of kings. It is an act of daring, as if a naked homeless pauper should spit in the face of his lawful king. O my reader, repeat not the terrible offense! Recognize the rights of your Creator, and crawl humbly to his feet, with tearful eyes, and with solemn resolutions of loyalty in time to come.

You are doubtless familiar with the story of the Macedonian soldier, who was shipwrecked and cast ashore by the waves, helpless, nude, and nearly dead. A farmer found him in this sad condition, and bore him from the beach to his home. There he laid him on his own bed, restored him to consciousness, nourished him, and for six weeks supplied all his wants with more than a brother's tenderness and liberality.

The soldier, restored to health and vigor by this affectionate care, and furnished with money for his journey by his liberal host, left the house of his benefactor, and went to the court of King Philip, That monarch, who knew the soldier to be a man of uncommon valor, received him with favor, listened with interest to the story of his misfortunes, and asked him what reward he craved for his services.

"Give me," said the unworthy warrior, "the lands which lie along the shore where I was wrecked!"

"They are yours," replied the prince; and thus the soldier became the owner of the estate of his benefactor. Armed with authority from the king, he returned to the house of his hospitable host, drove him from his home, and took possession of all his property.

The injured farmer took measures to inform King Philip of the services he had rendered his unprincipled guest, and of this most ungracious treatment. Fired with indignation at the unexampled ingratitude of the soldier, the monarch revoked his gift, restored the property to its true owner, seized the soldier, and caused the words "*Ungrateful Guest*" to be branded on his forehead.

Here is a fact of an opposite character. An aged gentleman, who had spent his life in the enjoyment of all the comforts and elegancies which abundant wealth can procure, met with an overwhelming misfortune, which, like a mighty flood, suddenly swept his property away. Reduced to poverty, he broke up his establishment and dismissed his domestics. Among his servants there was one who refused to quit him. She said:

"I have served you twenty-five years. You have treated me with the kindness of a master, a father, and a friend. To you, under God, I owe my life, my education, and the salvation of my soul. I cannot leave you. I have saved considerable money in your service. Accept it, and let me still serve you, trusting in Him who feedeth the ravens to provide for me should I ever become old and helpless."

The unfortunate old man wept, as well he might, on hearing these noble words. He took his servant's money and lived on it until the death of a relative restored him to competence. Then he returned the servant's gift with interest, and when he died further requited her gratitude by bequeathing her an ample maintenance.

Now review these facts and tell me what your feelings are toward the several parties? Does not your soul recoil with emotions of dislike, contempt, and horror from the conduct of the soldier toward his benefactor? On the contrary, does not your heart warm with strong approval of the grateful servant? But why do these opposite emotions swell your breast? Is it not because you are so constituted as to perceive, by simple intuition, that he who, being needy, is benefited by another, is under obligations to be grateful in heart and act to the benefactor who ministers to his necessities. The *soldier* violated this obligation, and therefore you instinctively abhor him; the *servant* respected it, and you as instinctively approve and admire her conduct.

Will you now apply this principle to yourself and the Creator? Is he not *your* benefactor? What but his goodness led him to give you being? He would be infinitely happy if his dominion was one vast, illimitable solitude, without a created voice to break its mysterious silence. Not for the increase of his own bliss, therefore, did he bring you into life; but he did it that you might taste the luxury of existence, and enjoy the happiness of knowing and loving him. Then, with what wonderful skill and beneficence he molded your form into beauty, and framed it so that the proper exercise of its functions is a constant source of pleasure! With what munificence he has provided objects of utility, beauty, and sublimity in the world for the supply of your wants, the gratification of your tastes, and the instruction of your understanding! With what fatherly love has his eye watched and his arm protected your life from the first moment of your existence until now! What unnumbered dangers he has averted from you! From what innumerable causes of death he has shielded you! How often has his invisible arm dragged you from the open jaws of ruin! How profusely has he poured earthly blessings and comforts into your lap! With what unspeakable condescension has he stooped to care for you, to sympathize with you, to make you an object of especial concern, though you are but as the "drop of a bucket" amid the amplitude and grandeur of his infinite dominion! Surely he is your benefactor, and you may very fitly lift your adoring eyes to his throne and say:

"Thou shin'st with everlasting rays;
Before the insufferable blaze
  Angels with both wings vail their eyes;
Yet free as air thy bounty streams;
On all thy works thy mercy's beams,
  Diffusive as thy sun's, arise.

"Astonish'd at thy frowning brow,
Earth, hell, and heaven's strong pillars bow;
Terrible majesty is thine!
Who then can that vast love express
Which bows thee down to me—who less
Than nothing am, till thou art mine!"

Yes, God *is* your benefactor indeed. The favors of all your human friends compared with his are but as the tiniest streams that trickle from mountain-sides to the oceans which girdle the globe. Standing thus related to him as a helpless dependant on an almighty benefactor, what is your duty? Say, poor worm, whose power to crawl in the light of the majestic sweetness which crowns his regal brow is derived from him—say, what OUGHT you do? OUGHT you not to return his benefactions by rendering him the ceaseless homage of a grateful heart, and the obedience which he has condescended to command in his holy word? Apart from all other considerations, is it not God's *right*, as your owner and benefactor, to require your service, and your *duty*, as his creature whom he has loaded with benefits, to declare with the Psalmist, "O Lord, truly I am thy servant?" I know that your conscience dictates an affirmative reply, and you cannot withhold your approval of the sentiment of the great CHALMERS, who says: "Only grant God to be our benefactor and our owner, and on this relation alone do we confidently found our obligations, both of love and gratitude."

During a heavy and long-continued gale of wind, accompanied with dense fog, the look-out at the bows of a ship shouted, "Breakers ahead!"

"Port your helm!" cried the captain to the steersman.

It was too late. Before the order could be obeyed the ship dashed upon a rock and became a helpless wreck. The boats were got out; most of the seamen and passengers crowded into them, while some leaped into the sea and swam for the shore, which was nigh. Among the passengers were a lady and her son, who were left uncared for until the last seaman was leaving the ship. Grasping the boy, he said: "There is room for you in the boat," and was about to lower him over the bulwarks.

But the boy tore himself from the sailor's grasp, and said: "Save my mother, if you have to let me drown!"

There was no time for hesitation or reflection. The mother was hurried into the boat. The boy leaped overboard and was happily picked up by the other boat and saved with the mother, who, but for his noble spirit of self-sacrifice, would have been left to perish on the wreck.

This fact may illustrate a great truth. Let it teach you that unusual benefits impose new and special obligations to gratitude and service on their recipients. It had always been that mother's duty to love and serve her son, because she was his mother; but after he, by his self-devotion, had saved her life, were not new obligations of gratitude and love imposed upon her? He was only her son before; afterward he was also her heroic deliverer—the saviour of her life, and she was therefore bound to him by a new tie.

And is not your Creator, owner, and benefactor, also your REDEEMER and SAVIOUR? Hear what Holy Scripture saith of him in this relation: He "bought" you "with a price." "He redeemed you not with corruptible things, as silver and gold . . . . but with the precious blood of Christ." He "so loved" you that "he gave his only-begotten Son" to be "wounded for your transgressions," "bruised" for your "iniquities." "He laid on him" your iniquity; the "chastisement" of your peace was upon him, and by "his stripes" you may be healed.

This redeeming act was God's most wonderful and infinite benefaction. Christ crucified was the richest gift in your Creator's possession; the highest possible demonstration of his exhaustless love! What greater thing can mind imagine than an Almighty Being giving his coequal Son to be incarnated and made to suffer as the substitute of a race of guilty creatures? What higher good could Deity offer to intelligent though sinful beings, than pardon, adoption, participation in his own moral beauty, and intimate fellowship with himself around the throne on which he chiefly manifests his person and glory? What more perfect demonstration of sincere solicitude for human happiness can be imagined than is found in the provisions of the Gospel? Look at them a moment.

As the basis of the system you have a Redeemer, whose sufferings stand accepted as the substitute foı the eternal damnation of as many as may choose to make him their hiding-place. Then, as the first-fruits of those sufferings, every child of Adam is held to be as guiltless at birth as though it had descended from sinless ancestors: to counteract that tendency to sinful self-indulgence which every child inherits, there is given to it, not an actually regenerated nature, but the presence of the Holy Spirit, seeking, in conjunction with its spiritual educators, to beget in it that affection for God which is the essence and principle of the regenerated life; to give long opportunity of being saved to those who waywardly resist "the grace of God which bringeth salvation," and contract the guilt of manifold sins, provision is made in Christ for the pardon of "*many offenses;*" to render this provision operative, there is a Divine revelation to instruct; a living ministry and a visible Church to proclaim the truth; a gracious influence from the Holy Spirit directly exercised upon the soul of the sinner, opening the eyes of his understanding, quickening his conscience, appealing to his affections, pressing, without forcing, his will, and infusing moral strength in every moment of awakened spiritual desire. Moreover, the conditions on which the great salvation is suspended are of the simplest character, and, with the spiritual help offered, the easiest of which the mind can conceive. They are not *arbitrary*, but *necessary* in themselves. How could guilt be pardoned without penitence? How could love be born and communion enjoyed without faith? Indeed it is difficult to conceive how God could have done more or required less for human salvation than he has in the Gospel of his Son. Well might the apostle exclaim: "Behold what manner of love the Father hath bestowed upon us!"

Say, therefore, thoughtful youth, does not this revelation of your Divine Benefactor, in the relation of Saviour and Redeemer, impose new obligations on you to love and serve him? If, as your *owner* and *benefactor*, his claims to your grateful service were indisputable and inextinguishable, what can you say to his right in you as your *Redeemer?* If ingratitude to a benefactor be infamous; if to deprive an owner of his right to control his property be robbery, by what epithet shall I designate the rejection of a *Saviour's* claims, the trampling under foot of a *Redeemer's* rights? It is a sin for which human language refuses to furnish a name; it is a monstrous combination of all that is vile in every other form of sin; it is the only sin for which souls are damned. "He that believeth not the Son shall not see life, but the wrath of God abideth upon him."

Come, then, thou creature of the Most High, thou helpless dependant upon thy Divine Benefactor, thou redeemed one, cast thyself at the feet of thy Lord, because he is thy Lord, thy Benefactor, and thy Redeemer! Because it is your DUTY, and not merely because your happiness requires it, give God your heart! You owe him service; render it because you owe it. You owe him gratitude; let your heart yield it because it is his right to claim it. You owe him your highest love, therefore place your heart in his willing hands, and "love him, because he has loved you." Bind yourself to him with chains of penitence, faith, and love, for the sake of what he is in himself, and not merely because his service will produce your highest happiness.

It is related of a certain monk that he once lighted upon an ancient chapel in a lonely forest. He entered it, and found its walls bare, and its stone altar crumbling with age and covered with mold. As his curious eyes scanned the pointed arches, they were arrested by a quaint-looking window above the altar, which, in the gloom, looked as if some unpracticed hand had smeared it with red paint. After gazing upon it a few moments the old man spoke and said:

"Fy! a blind man could paint as well with soot and blood. That daub is as meaningless as chaos."

The words had scarcely left his lips before the descending sun, bursting from an envious cloud, poured a flood of radiance upon the window. Thus lighted, what had seemed a daub in the previous gloom, resolved itself into a splendid painting. There, in life-like form, was Moses and the burning bush, with the stern rocks of Sinai and the snowy flocks of the noble shepherd quietly grazing on its rugged sides. The monk looked on the painted glass with wonder, and exclaimed:

"Ha! what a light! It has changed that motley stain to the product of a master artist's hand."

Now it may be, my reader, that my feeble attempts to portray the beauty of the Divine character have been to you as that painting was to the dim-eyed monk, while as yet the sun was clouded. Possibly you have never yet been impressed and thrilled by clear perceptions of the moral beauty, the peerless loveliness, of the moral nature of God. Like the wicked Jews, you see neither form nor comeliness in the manifestations which your Benefactor has made of himself. If this be so, let my illustration teach you that the fault is all in yourself. God is the perfection of beauty, the concentration of all moral loveliness. To see him thus you must study him as he is portrayed in his word. Let that book be to you what the church window was to the monk. Look into it with the teachable spirit of a little child, with unquestioning belief of its statements, with desire to discover the glory and excellency of its Author. Look thus constantly, patiently, earnestly, and it will not be long before the Sun of Righteousness will shed a flood of glorious light upon it. Then you will see the Divine character in such lovely aspects as will fill you with rapturous desire, and enable you to say with the Psalmist, "My heart and my flesh crieth out for the living God;" and with the poet:

> "Ever fainting with desire,
> For thee, O Christ, I call;
> Thee I restlessly require;
> I want my God, my all."

With such views and such desires you will be prepared to love and serve God for *the sake of what he is in himself*, and because he is Creator, Owner, Benefactor, and Redeemer to you, his dependent, helpless, sinful creature. I do not say you will cease to be influenced by the fact that godliness is, as I have shown, productive of your personal happiness; for it is only through his beneficent provisions for your happiness that you can attain to those perceptions of the loveliness of his character which can enrapture and captivate your affections. But I do affirm that the nearer you get to God the clearer and more far-seeing your visions of his moral perfections become, the less you will think of yourself, and the more powerfully you will be attracted by his beauty.

What more need be said? If piety be a river of perpetual happiness, invigorating the soul in its moral conflicts, refreshing it in its hours of weariness, solacing it in its days of gloom, satisfying its immortal thirstings, and fitting it for heavenly felicity; if its demands are the rights of God and your duties; if without it you must be eternally separated from God, and from all enjoyment, and doomed to suffer unspeakable woe, then, surely, the array of motives is perfect. Self-love and duty speak one language, and urge you to say to God, "My Father, from this time thou shalt be the guide of my youth."

Listen, then, I beseech you, to the voices of gratitude, love, and duty. By all that is sacred in your obligations to God; by all that is lovely in the Divine character; by all that is commanding in the authority and terrible in the justice of the Almighty; by all that is desirable in heaven and dreadful in hell; by the curses of the law; by the love, the sufferings, the tears, the blood of your long-neglected, despised, but faithful and patient Redeemer, I entreat you, beloved youth, to begin a life of piety this moment. Now inquire, with all the earnestness of which you are capable, "What shall I do to be saved?" Now pray with good old Francis Quarles, and say:

"Eternal God! O thou that only art
  The sacred fountain of eternal light,
And blessed loadstone of my better part;
  O thou, my heart's desire, my soul's delight!
Reflect upon my soul, and touch my heart,
  And then my heart shall prize no good above thee;
And then my soul shall know thee; knowing, love thee;
  And then my trembling thoughts shall never start
From thy commands, or swerve the least degree,
  Or once presume to move, but as they move in thee."

CHAPTER XII.

WHAT SHALL I DO TO BE SAVED?

More than a century ago a little orphan boy, scarcely seven years old, stood on a slight eminence, from which a lovely landscape met his eye. Broad fields of waving grain, extensive pastures stocked with fine breeds of cattle, a magnificent park with its herds of antlered deer quietly feeding in the shade of venerable oaks and elms which have withstood the storms of centuries, a cosy old manor-house, and a picturesque village with its thatched cottages and old stone church draped in ivy, were all included in the scene before him. Long and pensively did that boy gaze on this delightful spot of rural beauty, for he had heard his grandfather say that all those broad lands once belonged to his ancestors. But they had passed into the hands of strangers. His parents were dead. His grandfather was old and poor, and there was little in his life-prospects to awaken the voices of hope within his childish bosom. No wonder the thoughtful boy felt sad.

Presently, however, his tearful eye grew bright. His graceful little form stood erect and dignified. He trod the soil proudly and firmly. His whole person and manner showed that a great purpose was being born within him. He was resolving to become the master of that great estate!

From that moment the boy's character acquired fresh strength. That resolution beamed like a star upon his path and cheered him in every struggle. On he pressed through poverty, toil, discouragement, and trial. In every moment of despondency his resolution spurred him to renewed effort. Gradually at first, and rapidly at length, he acquired wealth and power, until he, the noted WARREN HASTINGS, became governor-general of India, and owner of Daylesford manor, his ancestral seat. He achieved his purpose.

Resolution is the parent of action. Hence, as young Warren Hastings resolved to recover the estate of his ancestors, so must you, my reader, firmly *resolve* to seek your soul's conversion before you can be saved. To this resolution I entreat you to come at once. Having in the previous chapters spread the facts and motives before you on which such a resolution must be based, I beg you to reduce the impressions you have received to a definite and operative purpose. Let me give you an example.

A gentleman, who was a magistrate and possessed great personal influence, was strongly urged, one evening, by his pious wife, to seek his soul's conversion *at once*. He listened long, without making a remark. At length he calmly replied, "I WILL!"

He spent much of that night in sober meditation. The next morning he was bowed down under a profound sense of guilt. Reflection on the past, aided by the Holy Spirit, had brought his conscience into a state of activity, and the depths of his nature were stirred with sorrow for sin.

At nine o'clock he started for a protracted meeting then being held a mile or two from his abode. On the way he prevailed on four of his friends—two lawyers, a brother magistrate, and a physician—to accompany him. Before reaching the church they paused at the residence of a judge, who was busy on his farm. "Judge," said the awakened man, "I am determined to seek the salvation of my soul. I have persuaded these, my neighbors, to accompany me. Come, lay aside your plow, and go along to meeting."

The judge remained silent awhile, then, looking at his friend, he said, "I will!"

The whole party proceeded to church. After the sermon they attended the inquiry meeting. The result was, that all but one of that party, in a short time, received the forgiveness of sins. The gentleman himself had a longer struggle before finding peace than either of his friends; but he persevered, and after a whole night spent in prayer, the grace of God burst like sunshine upon his heart, and he went on his way rejoicing.

I commend this resolute man's example to you, immortal youth. He started without much feeling. A clear intellectual perception of duty, such as you possess, led him to say irrevocably, "*I will seek God* NOW!" Acting under the guidance of that stern volition, he began at once to turn his thoughts to the consideration of his past life, of his relations to God, of his duty and destiny. That consideration gave birth to penitential emotion, for by it he turned his face toward God, whose Spirit at once shone upon his inmost nature and melted all its hardness into sorrow, as the sun melts the ice and snow of winter into streams of running water.

Now all this is possible with you. Your heart may be as cold and hard as a polar iceberg. It may be as barren of good desires as a desert is of fruit or flower. All its feelings may be concentrated in one absorbing consciousness of aversion against a religious life, nevertheless you can—such is the liberty of your will, aided as it is by the grace which bringeth salvation—you can now resolve, as that magistrate did, from a simple sense of duty, that you will seek to become a Christian. I appeal to your consciousness of power. Do you or do you not feel able to make that resolve? "I DO," is the instinctive response of your nature.

Yes, I know you do. And I also know that in this critical moment of your life, while all that is carnal within you shrinks with aversion from the decisive act, there is also a secret monitor whispering in the ear of your immortal spirit, and gently stimulating you to do it. That whisper is divine. It is the voice of the Eternal Spirit. It is Christ's latest voice of love. It is heaven's pledge to you, that if you will do violence to the aversion of your carnal mind by resolving to repent, you shall not be left to wage the mighty warfare alone. It is God, the ever faithful and true, saying, "Let the wicked forsake his way, and the unrighteous man his thoughts; and let him return unto the Lord, and he will have mercy upon him; and to our God, for he will abundantly pardon."

Heed it, O precious youth! Heed that voice of power. Make the decisive resolution *now*. Here it is. Read it:

BY THE GRACE OF GOD I WILL THIS INSTANT SEEK THE SALVATION OF MY SOUL.

Signed, ____________

Concentrate all the energy of your will into this great purpose. Let it be final, irreversible. Having formed it, set your name to it, and consider the question settled. Your back is upon the world, your face is heavenward. Henceforth you are to be a pilgrim to the city of Jesus.

Thank God! thank God! Let there be joy in the presence of the angels. Another soul has taken its first step in the pleasant pathway—another soul has turned its imploring glance toward the mercy-seat of God. For this let there be joy in heaven. It will not be long before there will be peace in the troubled breast of the seeker.

Now, my fellow-sinner, having made this solemn purpose, you must study yourself with introspective eye. But let me lead you to the only spot on earth where such a study can result in softening your heart. I mean to Calvary. Talk your meditations in whispered words addressed to the dying lover of souls. Look up! See that pale, blood-stained face! Majestic sweetness, amid all its traceries of woe, is written upon it. Behold it! That sufferer is making atonement for your sins. The pains which rend him, and the death he is dying, are the substitutes which your offended Creator has covenanted to accept, whenever you become a believer, instead of that eternal anguish which is the proper punishment of the sins you have committed. Love for you, therefore, sent him on his mission of suffering. Love for you sustains him in its endurance. "Behold the Lamb of God!" the "propitiation" for your sins, and while beholding meditate.

Your past life, what has it been? Rays of softest light beamed from that cross on your infant footsteps. Streams of richest benefactions have ever flowed from that opened side along the paths of your childhood and youth. Christian parents, pious teachers, an open Bible, freedom to worship God, a faithfully preached Gospel, voices of admonition from human lips and from the Divine Spirit, restraining grace, protective providences, blessings of the earth beneath and blessings of the heavens above, divine forbearance, patient long-suffering, with innumerable other mercies, have been freely lavished upon you in answer to his pleadings.

What returns have you made? Have you consulted your Divine benefactor respecting the use of his gifts? Rather, have you not received and expended his benefactions without the least regard to his will? Though an absolute pauper in your Creator's household, have you not used his favors with the independence of a sovereign? Has one grateful acknowledgment, one truly loving aspiration for his approval, ever burned on your selfish heart? Living in yourself and for yourself, have you not despised his authority and been a rebellious child? Besides leaving undone the duties he commanded, have you not done daily, hourly, in unnumbered instances, the things he has forbidden? Take his holy commandments and see if you have not, either in spirit or letter, broken them all? Instead of taking him for your one God, and loving him with all your heart, have you not had gods many and lords many? Have you not often spoken his name vainly, if not, indeed, profanely? Have you not broken his Sabbaths, disobeyed your parents, and, by cherishing hatred, been guilty of murder in your heart? By indulging lustful desires — and it may be by actual personal pollution — have you not trampled on the law which forbids adultery? Has no act of fraud, such as dishonest bankruptcy, fraudulent dealing, or downright theft, arrayed the eighth commandment against you? Has not a lie often defiled your lips, and covetousness your mind? To which then of the ten commandments can you plead, "I am not guilty?" Alas for you! your past life is covered with transgression. It is written all over with rebellion, self-indulgence, pride, ingratitude, and sins of every hue. "*Is not thy wickedness great?*" and are not "*thine iniquities infinite?*"

Drag this black past into the light. View it on every side. Count, if you can, the number of your transgressions. Ascertain their turpitude. Remember that they have been committed against Him whom you saw bleeding on the cross for you and such as you. See how sadly he gazes at you while all his bleeding wounds are saying, "Soul! soul! why sinnest thou against thy Redeemer and friend?"

Consider, also, that your long resistance to the pleadings of Christ's precious love affords conclusive proof of the exceeding wickedness of your heart. You strongly resemble a youth who fell into the snares of dissipation, and fled to a distant city that he might indulge in folly without rebuke. Anxious for his welfare, his father sent an only brother to woo him back to home and virtue. The brother was repelled with rudeness. His sister was next sent, but he turned away unmoved from her pure words of love. His patriarchal father then tried the power of paternal persuasion, but even his gray hairs and breaking heart failed to melt the stubborn youth. Last of all, his venerable mother, trembling with age and infirmities, traveled to his haunts, and besought him, with all the touching pathos of maternal love, to forsake his vices and return to the happy home he had abandoned. Vainly she pleaded, for even his mother's tears had no power to charm him from his darling vices.

Now tell me frankly, my dear reader, which part of this youth's conduct most clearly proves his depravity, his first dissipations or his persistent resistance to the wooings of his family ?

His persistent resistance? You answer truly, and by so doing convict yourself of wickedness as deeply rooted as your inmost nature, and as vile as ever stained a human soul; for as that youth resisted every effort of parental and fraternal love, so have you, through all the years of your life, resisted all the efforts of Divine love to win your heart to righteousness. In vain have voices of parental love, of teachers and pastors, of the inspired book, of your own consciences, of the Holy Spirit, and of the interceding Saviour entreated you. In vain have the love of God and the tears of Jesus, the terrors of justice and the gifts of mercy, made their appeals to your wicked heart. You have steadfastly resisted them all. If, therefore, unconquerable resistance to redeeming efforts is the strongest proof of inveterate wickedness, you must be wicked indeed. You may not have the blot of open immorality staining your life, but you have shown an aversion to God as strong as that which rules the heart of the vilest wretch who walks the earth! Indeed, I know not but that your aversion is stronger than his, for he has rioted in sin away from Gospel influences, while you have sinned in sight of Calvary! Had he enjoyed one half the sweet influences which have crowned your life, possibly he would have repented long ago. But *you!* You have lived an irreligious life in the very ante-chamber of the Divine presence; you have resisted the uttermost efforts of Divine compassion. "Is not your wickedness great?"

Shrink not from these painful views of yourself, precious soul, but drag all your sinfulness to the light. Confess it all to Him who was "bruised" for your "iniquities." Acknowledge all you transgressions. Make no excuses. Palliate no act of your life; but, gazing at the cross, abase yourself, crying with the publican, "God be merciful to me a sinner," and with the prodigal, "Father, I have sinned."

These meditations and confessions will bring the Holy Spirit nearer to you, who will make your understanding light, your heart soft, unsealing all the springs of penitence within you, and enabling you to say with the poet:

"Awaked from sin's delusive sleep,
My heavy guilt I feel, and weep;
Beneath a weight of woes oppress'd,
I come to thee, my Lord, for rest."

It may be, however, that these purposes, meditations, and confessions will fail to melt your heart. Burdened, tempest-tossed, dark, without tender feeling, and full of unbelief, you may make no seeming progress. If this be so, despair not. The cloud lowers around the cross only because you are clinging to some sin which you are not willing to give up at the command of Christ. You may be but dimly conscious of this unwillingness. To test yourself put up this prayer:

"What is it keeps me back,
From which I cannot part—
Which will not let the Saviour take
Possession of my heart?
Searcher of hearts, in mine
Thy trying power display;
Into its darkest corners shine,
And take the vail away."

That you may know the mind of God respecting your favorite sins, consider these words: "If the wicked restore the pledge, *give again that he had robbed, walk in the statutes of life without committing iniquity*, he shall surely live, he shall not die."

This passage is a torch lighted at the altar of God's purity. Hold it up in your heart, and learn that if you would approach God acceptably, you must make no secret mental compromise with sin. IF YOU HAVE EVER WRONGED ANY MAN BY CHEATING, BY THEFT, OR BY BANKRUPTCY, YOU MUST MAKE RESTITUTION—"*give again that he had robbed*;" if you are in a sinful business, such as rum-selling, trading or working on the Sabbath, slaveholding, slave-trading, grinding the poor by oppressive wages, or any other practice which violates the laws of God or man, you must unconditionally, and at once, abandon it, or you cannot find that Divine favor which is conditioned on your consent "*to walk in the statutes of life* WITHOUT COMMITTING INIQUITY." You may mentally spare some profitable sin, and may so persuade your conscience into a compromise with it, as to patch up a spurious peace with God and become a member of the Church; but such repentance, and such peace will not stand when God maketh inquisition for sin. His righteous arm will tear away your mask in that terrible day, and after revealing your hideous deformities, he will say: "*I never knew you; depart from me*, YE THAT WORK

INIQUITY." Remember that all repentance is spurious which does not lead you to give up every known sin.

That you may see how the Spirit of God teaches truly awakened souls, I will submit three pertinent facts. The first relates to the duty of *restitution.*

A gentleman once saw a captain, with whom he was about to sail as a passenger, carelessly throw a bag of dollars on a locker. By way of alarming the captain, the gentleman hid the money. It happened that in the hurry of leaving port the reception of the bag of dollars entirely faded from the captain's recollection, and the gentleman carried it ashore, intending to return it when it should be missed. But months passed before inquiry was made, and then the gentleman, fearing lest his honesty should be questioned, purposely secreted the money. Meanwhile the captain was sued for the amount, and imprisoned. Confinement and vexation killed him, and his wife and children were left penniless.

The hand of God now touched the gentleman and he became fatally sick. The voice of God alarmed his conscience. Hell gat hold upon his spirit. He sent for Dr. Adam Clarke, and guided by his spiritual counsels, earnestly sought pardon and peace. But he sought in vain. Prayers, tears, and sorrow brought no comfort to his tormented soul. At length, being closely questioned by Dr. Clarke, he confessed his theft of the bag of dollars.

"*You must make restitution!*" said that holy man. "You can restore the money, and redeem the dead man's memory from infamy!"

The dying man consented, and restored the money with compound interest. Then his prayers were heard, and his long agonized spirit soon found rest in Jesus.

Penitent reader, have you ever wronged any man of his property? Have the wages of unrighteousness ever defiled your conscience? If so, you must "give again what you have robbed," or make up your mind to be shut out of that heaven into which "*there shall in no wise enter anything that defileth.*" Be not deceived. "God is not mocked." He who is not willing to make restitution to the utmost of his ability, is not truly sorry for having perpetrated the injustice which he is required, as far as possible, to undo.

My second fact relates to the sin of slaveholding,

and is taken from the life of that spiritual hero, Freeborn Garrettson. A few hours after his conversion a strange and terrible darkness overspread his spirit. He was in agony, though he knew not why. At length, while conducting family prayer, God showed him his reason for hiding his face. As he was reading a hymn this thought powerfully struck his mind:

"It is not right for you to keep your fellow-creatures in bondage; you must let the oppressed go free!"

Mr. Garrettson had never heard slaveholding condemned until that moment. He had never read a book on the subject, but his conscience at once recognized the Divine authority of that powerful thought. He paused a moment. Being thoroughly in earnest, he only wished to know what God willed. Satisfied on this point, he exclaimed:

"Lord, the oppressed shall go free!"

Having formed this hallowed purpose, he at once said to his slaves: "You do not belong to me. I do not desire your services without making you a compensation." Speaking of the effect of this act of justice on his own heart, he says:

"All my dejection, and that melancholy gloom which preyed upon me, vanished in a moment, and a divine sweetness ran through my whole frame!"

Penitent reader, are you a slaveholder? Protected by impious laws, are you holding immortal, responsible, and naturally free-born men, women, and children in the condition of personal chattels? Are you rearing the purchase of the Redeemer's blood as you rear cattle, for your own personal comfort and profit? If so, "I have a message from God unto thee." Here it is. Speaking to those who affect to repent without giving up their sins, God says: "Is not this the fast that I have chosen? to loose the bands of wickedness, to undo the heavy burdens, and to let the oppressed go free, and that ye break every yoke?" "Then shall thy light break forth as the morning, and thine health shall spring forth speedily."

My third fact relates to a distiller, who was powerfully awakened while at a religious assembly away from home. Like a flash of lightning a conviction of the sinfulness of his business, gleamed upon his heart. Speaking to himself, he said:

"If I seek religion I must give up my distillery. If I give that up I shall beggar my family. If I do not seek religion I can make a good living, but my soul must go to hell!"

After weighing the momentous question in his heart, and carefully counting the cost of the act, he went to the altar and put up this simple prayer:

"Lord, I will trust my family to thy care and seek the salvation of my soul. O Lord, I have built a still-house which I know I must give up before thou wilt pardon my sins, but I want the pardon of my sins to-night, for before to-morrow I may be dead. Lord, if thou wilt trust me, and for the sake of thy Son's death forgive my sins to-night, I will go home to-morrow morning, if spared, and knock every tub to staves, throw out the still, and never make another drop of liquor!"

That prayer was answered, and the peace which is more precious than money came into his soul. As he afterward remarked, "God saw my sincerity and converted my soul on credit." The still was destroyed. The man found ample compensation for his pecuniary sacrifices in the consciousness of duty performed and in the smile of his Creator. And so do all who, like him, follow the teachings of Christ and enter the gate of regeneration, casting away their former sins.

What say you to this, penitent soul? If engaged in any sinful business will you obey God, or, consulting your present gains only, will you follow corrupt popular example and your own selfish impulses? If the latter is your deliberate purpose, I have only to say that "whatsoever a man soweth, that shall he also reap." If you will sow to the flesh you must be content to "reap corruption." But, believe me, corruption is a shocking crop to harvest. But if your purpose is to keep the "statutes of life," then shall "thy light rise in obscurity, and thy darkness be as the noonday."

Do you still hesitate to decide between the profits of sin and the favor of God? Like a bird hopping between two twigs, are you yet in doubt as to which you will choose? O shameful indecision! Are virtue, happiness, heaven, and God so light in your esteem that they cannot weigh down the profits of sin? Let the conduct of a noble heathen bring a blush to your cheeks and put an end to such unworthy indecision.

When the Macedonian PYRRHUS was negotiating a treaty with FABRICIUS the Roman general, he offered to make that heroic man richer than the richest man in Rome, provided he would promise to influence the Roman senate in favor of his plans. Fabricius, who was as poor as he was brave, instantly replied:

"My little field, poor and unfertile as it is, supplies me with all that nature requires. If riches had been my ambition, I could have amassed great sums from the spoils of those enemies of Rome whom I have conquered. After this, would it now become me to accept the gold and silver you offer me? What example should I set the citizens of Rome? How could I bear even their looks at my return? You shall then, if you please, keep your riches to yourself, and I will keep my poverty and my reputation!"

Incorruptible Fabricius! He counted his honor worth more than much gold. The treasures of a king could not kindle in his noble nature even a desire to swerve from his duty to his country. Beside his nobility of soul, how mean your hesitation to choose between the profits of a sinful business and your duty to God appears! Cursed be that lust of gold which keeps you from the cross of Christ! What will those sin-stained profits avail when your soul is lost? Will they not follow you, woven into a poisoned garment, and like the shirt of Nessus on the back of Hercules, torment you with unspeakable pain forever? Be resolute, therefore, and in the spirit of the distiller and of Freeborn Garrettson, for your soul's sake, yield every sinful pursuit with all its accursed profits, and God will give you a "hundred-fold" in this world, and you "shall inherit everlasting life."

Assuming that you are purposed to give up all participation in sinful practices or in sinful business, however profitable, I advise you to believe in the Lord Jesus Christ. Being sorry for sin, and willing to forsake it, there is nothing more required of you but to believe. You may not be able to shed many tears; that depends very much on the peculiarity of your mental constitution; yet I say unto you, "Behold the Lamb of God." God sets more value on a single sincere purpose to forsake sin, or one hour's actual abandonment of wrong-doing, than he would on an Atlantic of tears if you were able to weep them. Look not, then, at your tears nor at your feelings, but at your regrets and purposes. Are you sorry that you have sinned? Do you truly regret that you have so long lived in the habit of resisting the grace of Christ? Are you resolved to "go and sin no more?" If so, "believe on the Lord Jesus Christ and thou shalt be saved." Send up your imploring cry to heaven, saying:

> "Jesus, Lord, my heart will break,
> Save me for thy great love's sake."

For explanations and illustrations of saving faith you may consult the following chapter.

CHAPTER XIII.

THE FAITH THAT SAVES US.

In the hall of an emperor's palace a trembling girl once cast herself at the monarch's feet and said:

"Pardon, sire! pardon for my father!"

"Who is your father?" inquired Napoleon; "and who are you?"

"I am Miss Lajolais, and, sire, my father is doomed to die!"

"Ah, young lady," replied Napoleon, "I can do nothing for you. This is the second time your father has conspired against the state. It is just that he should die!"

"Alas!" cried the girl, weeping bitterly; "I know it, sire; but the first time papa was innocent. To-day I do not ask for justice—I implore pardon, pardon for my father!"

The emperor's lips trembled and his piercing eyes filled with tears. Recovering himself, he gave the maiden his hand and said: "Well, my child, for your sake I will pardon your father!"

Not justice but pardon! That is precisely what you need at the hands of God, penitent youth! Justice would consign you to devouring flames. You need, NOT JUSTICE—BUT PARDON.

You also need a renewed heart. Without that, if pardoned, you would go on sinning as before. But your heavenly Father has provided for that necessity. In the moment of your pardon the Holy Spirit will "shed the love of God abroad" in your heart. That love is the principle of regeneration, the vital element of a new life, by means of which you will possess both disposition and ability to keep the commandments of God.

PARDON, therefore, is the great gift which you are to seek. And pardon is promised to all them that believe on the name of Jesus. "Whosoever believeth in him shall receive remission of sin." What, then, is that faith by which you are to obtain pardon? The following illustration will make it plain.

Through twelve weary years a poor woman had been the victim of a wasting disease. She had made herself penniless by her outlays in searching for health. The most skillful physicians had pronounced her incurable, and despair had built its throne in her heart.

But one day there came into her city a man whose fame had spread over all the land. He had healed multitudes of sick. He had never failed to cure the most stubborn case of disease. He had even raised the dead, and commanded the powers of nature like a God. Hearing of his arrival the woman's hopes revived again. "He has cured others," she thought, "he can cure me. He has never refused to put forth his power, he will therefore put it forth for me. If I can but see him I shall be cured!"

Thus believing in the power and love of JESUS, she sought him in the crowded street. Feeble but resolute, she edged her way through the living mass. But after using her utmost effort she could only get behind him, but not so as to catch his eye or ear. Then she said in her heart, "I will touch the border of his garment and that will be sufficient to heal me." Forcing her arm between the persons who stood next to the Saviour, she touched the border of his garment, expecting to feel the tides of returning health flow through her wasted form at once. And it was so.

In that moment a delightful consciousness of perfect health awoke within her. The suffering invalid was suddenly transformed into a healthy and vigorous woman.

Jesus, whose omniscient eye read all that passed in her heart, set his seal on this woman's faith, when, turning to her, he confirmed her cure by saying, "Daughter, be of good comfort; thy faith hath made thee whole; go in peace." Her faith may therefore be safely regarded as an example of that faith by which we are saved.

If you will review the history of this woman's case you will see (1.) that she despaired of recovery from any other source within or without herself; (2.) that she believed most implicitly in the love and power of Jesus; and (3.) that, firmly relying in her heart upon his power and love, she touched him, expecting an instant cure.

Such is the faith which brings pardon to a penitent sinner's heart. Like the woman, he approaches Christ, abandoning all trust in his own righteousness, and firmly believing that God, faithful to his promises, will pardon all who come to him in the name of Christ. Then, still following her example, he fixes his mental eye on Jesus, the mediator, and touching the border of his garment, says in his heart: "I take thee, O Christ, to be my Saviour. I trust in thy blood as the substitute for my eternal punishment. I rely on thy death for pardon. I am thy redeemed one. Thou art *my* Saviour. Thy blood prevails. It washes all *my* sins away." Thus leaning steadfastly on Christ, expecting instant peace, the penitent becomes suddenly conscious of a sweet calm stealing over his conscience. His previous depression floats away like the morning mist. A strange warmth is begotten in his heart. Christ becomes unspeakably precious to him, and he feels an inward prompting to look to God and fondly cry, "Abba, Father! *my* Lord, *my* God, *my* Redeemer!" "Being justified, he has *peace* with God through Jesus Christ."

This is faith, saving faith. It is very easy, very simple, to the truly contrite who cease all vain reasonings and, like the feeble invalid, make it their single purpose to touch the Saviour's garment and rely upon his love. Nevertheless, since unbelief is often very stubborn, I will further illustrate the nature of the faith which saves us.

In the highlands of Scotland there is a mountain-gorge twenty feet in width and two hundred feet in depth. Its perpendicular walls are bare of vegetation save in their crevices, in which grow numerous wild flowers of rare beauty. Desirous of obtaining specimens of these mountain beauties, some scientific tourists once offered a Highland boy a handsome gift if he would consent to be lowered down the cliff by a rope, and would gather a little basketful for them. The boy looked wishfully at the money, for his parents were poor; but when he gazed at the yawning chasm he shuddered, shrunk back, and declined. But filial love was strong within him, and after another glance at the gift and at the terrible fissure, his heart grew strong, his eyes flashed, and he said:

"I'll go *if my father will hold the rope!*"

And then, with unshrinking nerves, cheek unblanched, and heart firmly strong, he suffered his father to put the rope about him, lower him into that wild abyss, and to suspend him there while he filled his little basket with the coveted flowers. It was a daring deed, but his faith in the strength of his father's arm and in the love of his father's heart gave him courage to attempt and power to perform it.

This boy's trust is a beautiful illustration of the

faith which saves the soul; for as he put himself into his father's hands to be bound with the rope and lowered down the gorge to pluck the coveted flowers, so must you put yourself into Christ's hands to be pardoned. Binding yourself with the promises of God's mercy, you must give yourself into Christ's hands to be lowered into that depth of self-abasement where grows in peerless beauty the sweet flower of forgiveness. And when your feet are removed from all human grounds of hope, when all consciousness of self-righteousness is gone from within you, then, as that boy found courage, and peace, and strength in thinking, "My father knows this rope is strong; my father is able to hold it; my father loves me too well to let me fall," so will you find pardon, peace, and power in thinking, "My Father in heaven will not break this promise of mercy with which I have bound myself to him. He holds it in his hands. He loves me. He will not let his promise go. He saves me for Christ's sake!"

Try this faith, penitent youth, and it will save thee as surely as that boy's father held him firmly and drew him safely from the mountain gorge.

A little girl who once heard this incident related

as an illustration of faith, perceived the truth it ex plained, and found peace in believing. She was a delicate child, a pale mountain-flower, and soon drooped before the rude blasts which swept the hills among which she dwelt. She drew near the gates of death, and with smiles of seraphic sweetness awaited their opening. Loving eyes are fixed upon her as she reaches the moment of departure. When lo! they see her thin white arms spread out as if in search of something.

"What are you feeling after, my child?" tenderly inquires her weeping mother.

"I am feeling for the rope—the rope which Jesus holds. I've got it now. He is pulling! I am going!" is her beautiful reply.

Her hands close. An angelic smile plays upon her thin lips, a shout of rapturous joy breaks from her tongue, and she is gone. Fastened to the rope that Jesus holds, she is lifted into heaven!

How simple was that child's trust. Yet it was the faith that saves. God's promise to save "whosoever believeth" is the rope which Jesus holds. You have but to bind it about you by a mental act, to lie calmly recumbent upon it, saying: "This is Christ's promise sealed with his blood. He will not break it. He will keep it. He will raise me out of this pit of gloomy guilt, and place my feet upon a rock. He is pulling it now! I am pardoned!" and you will surely find mercy. The tempest in your heart will be hushed, and your quieted soul will be calm as heaven.

Take another illustration. A pious king was once taken sick. A prophet was sent from God to inform him that his sickness was unto death. Anxious for longer life, the royal patient offered a prayer of faith to God and was heard. Fifteen years were added to his life, and the prophet was sent to heal him. "Let them take a lump of figs and lay it for a plaster upon the boil and he shall recover," said the prophetic messenger.

In firm reliance upon the virtue which the power of God was to impart to this simple remedy, the king applied it to his wound and recovered. And a similar reliance upon the blood of Christ as the means of healing your guilty soul, my reader, is the faith that saves. To use the homely phrase of THOMAS WATSON, you must by a mental act "spread the sacred medicine of his blood upon your soul," saying as you do it, "Heal my soul for I have sinned," and looking, while you pray, for the removal of the pain of guilt from your conscience, and for the springing up of that sweet peace in your heart which is the sure result of an unmixed faith in the blood of Christ, and you will be justified.

The following incident contains a singular but beautiful conception of faith.

"What is the foundation of your hope?" said a minister to a sick native of a South Sea isle.

"O," he replied, "I saw an immense mountain with precipitous sides, on which I tried to climb; but when I reached a considerable height I lost my hold and fell to the bottom. Sad and fatigued, I went to a distance and sat down to weep. While weeping I saw a drop of blood fall upon that mountain, and in a moment it was dissolved. That mountain was my sins, and the drop which fell upon it was *one drop of the precious blood of Jesus*, by which the mountain of my guilt must be melted away."

Still another conception of justifying faith is contained in the following passage from the life of a devoted servant of Christ.

When that eminently holy man, the Rev. Charles

SIMEON, was seeking Christ, he groped as in Cimmerian darkness through three long months of bitter grief for sin. At length he read this remark in a sermon by Bishop Wilson: "The Jews knew what they did when they transferred their sin to the head of their offering."

These simple words shed a flood of light upon his heart. He saw that just as the scape-goat carried away the sins of the Jews, so Jesus takes away the sins of those who trust in him for that purpose. Seeing this he cried out:

"What! may I transfer all my guilt to another? Has God provided an offering for me that I may lay my sins on his head? Then, God willing, I will not bear them on my own soul one moment longer."

Thus Mr. Simeon cast his sins on the head of Christ, believing that they would no longer be charged against him. What was the result? The gloom of his soul dispersed. The tempest in his heart was calmed. The smile of Jesus beamed with hourly increasing brightness upon his spirit, and a few mornings after he awoke shouting: "Jesus Christ is risen to-day! Hallelujah! Hallelujah!"

"From that hour," as he testifies, "peace flowed *in rich abundance* into my soul. I had the sweetest access to God through my blessed Saviour!"

All these different conceptions of faith are but so many different modes of expression, either of which may be chosen by a penitent if it will aid him in exercising that inward, undoubting, unyielding reliance upon Christ for present pardon, which is the essence of true faith. You may claim him as your scape-goat carrying your sins into the wilderness; you may look at his blood as falling on your sins and melting them away; you may regard his blood as medicine healing your soul, while by a mental act you spread it upon yourself; you may bind yourself with his promise as to the rope which Jesus holds, expecting him to raise you up to the rock which is higher than you; you may put yourself into God's hands to be lowered into the vale of abasement, in which the flower of pardon grows; or you may touch the border of his garment,—it is all one, only be sure that you rely on the merit of Christ *alone* for present pardon.

On Christ only! Mark that word ONLY! and that you may understand its significance, read the following illustration:

An ancient allegory describes two boys, who, having to cross a morass by a dangerous path, stood trembling, and fearing to attempt it unaided. A strong man, with loving aspect, offers to conduct them. Placing himself between them, and offering each a hand, he said to them, "*Put your hands in mine!*"

One of the boys obeyed, and placed his hand in the open palm of his guide. The other said, "Not so, sir. I will take your hand in mine. I am strong, and can cling to you firmly, if we meet with danger."

Thus joined to their guide, they began their journey over the marsh. At first the path was wide enough for the three to walk abreast. Gradually it grew narrower, until it became a mere ridge barely sufficient for one person to tread upon. On either side a deep ditch yawned upon the travelers. Then the boys trembled. Having no foothold, their safety depended entirely on their hold upon the friendly guide. The boy who had refused to put his hand in the guide's, soon found himself unable to hold on to the hand he grasped. His muscles and joints were not strong enough to bear his weight, and, after several painful struggles, his fingers relaxed their grasp, and he fell into the ditch and perished. The other boy, having his hand in that of his powerful guide, was borne along in perfect safety. The hand that held him was mighty to save, and he soon found himself on safe and solid ground beyond the dreaded morass.

Let this allegory teach you, that in coming to God for pardon you must put yourself into Christ's hand, just as the latter boy put his hand into the guide's. You must rely for forgiveness *solely* on the fact that he died for you. That is putting yourself into Christ's hands. If you mix with that reliance a secret trust in your personal excellences, or in the merit of your own repentance, you will be *taking hold of his hand* instead of *putting your hand into his.* That trust in yourself will prevent the victory of your faith. Your personal excellences are lighter than flecks of foam in God's sight. Repentance has no merit. Faith has no merit. They are required because they imply states of mind which are essential to a saving reception of Christ. *Christ's blood alone saves.* "Not by works of righteousness which we have done, but according to his mercy he saved us," says the inspired apostle. Your faith must, therefore, turn away from every thought of merit in yourself, and fix its eye on Christ alone, saying, with a certain poor sailor:

"I'm a poor sinner and nothing at all;
But Jesus Christ is my all and in all."

Or, with the more elegant, but equally orthodox, poet:

"*Just as I am*, without one plea
But that Thy blood was shed for me,
And that Thou bidd'st me come to thee,
O Lamb of God, I come!

"*Just as I am*, and waiting not
To rid myself of one dark blot,
To Thee, whose blood can cleanse each spot,
O Lamb of God, I come!

"*Just as I am*, poor, wretched, blind,
Sight, riches, healing of the mind,
Yea, all I need in Thee to find,
O Lamb of God, I come!

"*Just as I am* thou wilt receive,
Wilt welcome, pardon, cleanse, relieve;
Because Thy promise I believe,
O Lamb of God, I come!

"*Just as I am*, Thy love unknown
Has broken every barrier down;
Now to be Thine, yea, Thine alone,
O Lamb of God, I come!"

Now then, beloved penitent, having shown you what faith is, and having guarded you against mixing the dross of self-righteousness with your trust in Christ, let me exhort you to believe at once—*just as you are.* Your heart may seem very hard, very dark, very wicked; all sorts of fears may be trembling within it, and you may appear to yourself to be at an infinite distance from Christ. Be it all so and worse, I, nevertheless, assure you, that if you have solemnly covenanted to give up all sin and to accept pardon from the lips of Jesus, as God's free unmerited gift, *you are on the threshhold of the kingdom of God.* Only believe, and you will be saved this instant! Look up! the Saviour is close to thee. Touch the hem of his garment! Say in your heart, "He healeth my soul." Hold firmly to that confidence! O how sweet it is to trust! Don't you feel it so? Does a sweet calm steal over your heart while you confide in him? Does Christ appear more precious to thee than life? Does the Holy Spirit move thee to cry, Abba, father? If so, joy to thee, my brother in Christ, thou art saved! That calm is the peace of God. That love to Christ is the divinely born principle of regeneration. Thou art saved! That cry is begotten by the Spirit witnessing your adoption. Glory be to God's holy name! O rejoice! rejoice!

Sing with the prophet, "O Lord, I will praise thee: though thou wast angry with me, thine anger is turned away, and thou comfortest me. Behold, God is my salvation; *I will trust, and not be afraid*, for the Lord JEHOVAH is my strength and my song; he also is become my salvation."

Should any lingering doubts assail you, do not cast away your new-born confidence, nor give way to idle reasonings, but *repeat the act of faith!* Put your soul into Christ's hands in the spirit of the Highland boy, and keep it there. Say to Him: "I commit my poor soul into thy hands, O blessed Jesus, to be pardoned, renewed, and saved. I am *persuaded* thou dost now accept and save me according to thy faithful word, and that thou wilt keep me in the possession of thy favor. I am *thine*, and thou, O blessed Jesus, art MINE forever." Let nothing induce thee to surrender this inward persuasion, and, depend upon it, Christ will honor it and comfort you.

If you are still in doubt, ponder the following hymn. Read it line by line. Adopt its thoughts and words for your own. Yield your heart to its teachings, and it will lead you to a manifested and pardoning Saviour:

"Arise, my soul, arise;
Shake off thy guilty fears;
The bleeding Sacrifice
In my behalf appears;
Before the throne my Surety stands,
My name is written on his hands.

"Five bleeding wounds he bears,
Received on Calvary;
They pour effectual prayers,
They strongly plead for me:
Forgive him, O forgive, they cry,
Nor let that ransom'd sinner die.

"The Father hears him pray,
His dear anointed One:
He cannot turn away
The presence of his Son:
His Spirit answers to the blood,
And tells me I am born of God.

"My God is reconciled;
His pard'ning voice I hear;
He owns me for his child;
I can no longer fear:
With confidence I now draw nigh,
And Father, Abba, Father, cry."

And now, beloved youth, having guided you to your Saviour and mine, I must bid you farewell. When you took up this little book you were an heir of hell. Now, if you have heeded my counsels, you are saved by faith. Give God the glory and persevere in well-doing. You will have difficulties, but God will give you grace to overcome them.* Only hold fast the beginning of your confidence, fight a good fight, keep the faith, let not sin defile your garments, and God will "keep thee from the hour of temptation," and give thee to "eat of the tree of life which is in the midst of the paradise of God." May it be your lot and mine to swell the number which have washed their robes in the blood of the Lamb, and to enjoy, in sweet, inseparable companionship, "the rest which remaineth for the people of God!"

* The difficulties and temptations to which the young Christian is exposed are fully explained and illustrated in "*The Path of Life*," by the author of this volume. The reader will find much to encourage him in that work, which is earnestly commended to his consideration as a fitting sequel to this.

THE END.

www.ingramcontent.com/pod-product-compliance
Lightning Source LLC
LaVergne TN
LVHW010216110826
845151LV00004B/1103

9781425527181